£2

CORRYMEELA
THE SEARCH FOR PEACE

CORRYMEELA

-----THE SEARCH FOR PEACE

ALF McCREARY

CHRISTIAN JOURNALS LIMITED
BELFAST.

First English edition 1975 by Christian Journals
Limited, 2 Bristow Park, Belfast BT9 6TH

Copyright © Christian Journals Limited 1975

ISBN 0 904302 15 6

Cover and illustrations by Rowel Friers.

Made and printed in Ireland by Cahill & Co, Dublin

**TO
HILARY**

Contents

Foreword

by
The Most Reverend Donald Coggan
Archbishop of Canterbury

The duration of my only visit to Corrymeela was extremely brief, fitted in between other engagements. But my memories of the visit are as vivid as the duration was short. Bright blue sky and sea, keen piercing wind, brilliant sunshine — all these things left an indelible impression of natural beauty.

Even more vivid is the memory of a small boy (off the streets of Belfast, I think) hugging a new-born lamb from the field nearby. Pity the lamb — it was having a rough time! But the boy — it was probably his first sight of any such thing. His world was a world of stones and guns and fire and slaughter. Corrymeela had brought him out from that, to meet with others of his own age and older than he, to discover that whatever their label, Protestant or Catholic, they were human beings, and to glimpse perhaps that they, like him, were made in the image of God.

Because Corrymeela is doing a work of reconciliation at a point where it is greatly needed, I count it a privilege to commend this book.

Lambeth Palace
September, 1975

Donald Cantuar:

They Came

Corrymeela is a large white building which stands near the edge of a clifftop on the North Coast of Ireland. It overlooks a scene of incomparable beauty, with the waves far below breaking on to the rocky strand and beyond that the sea stretching away to the shores of Scotland and the far North. On a hot summer's day with the sun glinting off the sea and the smell of the wild flowers in the fields beyond the house, Corrymeela is a haven of beauty and peace. It is almost inconceivable that Corrymeela is only 55 miles from Belfast and the scenes of some of the bitterest fighting in Europe since World War II.

Directly opposite Corrymeela lies the island of Rathlin, remote across the dangerous currents of the North Channel. This narrow strip of water has held the key to much history. It has helped to shape the two sides of Ireland. Symbolically and directly, Corrymeela looks over that channel which has borne the best and the worst of humanity since time began. The Vikings in their great longboats sailed past Corrymeela to pillage the island of Rathlin as a base for their forays to the Irish mainland. Saint Columba and

his followers sailed past Corrymeela hugging the coast in his frail coracle until he could slip across the treacherous swirls to the Mull of Kintyre and from thence to Iona which became the centre of Christian mission not only for Scotland but for the whole of Europe. And it was Ballycastle, the town beside Corrymeela, that Guglielmo Marconi and his aides used as a base to transmit the first wireless messages across that channel of water to Rathlin. Corrymeela symbolically was associated with the first revolutionary steps in wireless telegraphy that later was to bring men and women all over the world into closer communication.

Today Corrymeela continues to symbolize and to foster communication of a different kind. Corrymeela is more than a huge white house on a beautiful clifftop. It is a community of people, a concept in reconciliation, a way of life. Corrymeela and the Corrymeela Community is dedicated to fostering better understanding between all kinds of men and women not only in Ireland but far beyond. It is not a community of naive do-gooders. Its attitude is as sharp and refreshing as the winds that buffet its buildings from the cold realities of the sea far below.

Corrymeela was conceived and established before the recent years of violence opened all the old wounds in Ireland and thrust the horrors of the Irish conflict into the headlines of newspapers and newscasts in almost every country in the world. Corrymeela was overtaken by events, but not overwhelmed by them. For ten years Corrymeela has opened its doors to all comers—to the tired, the maimed, the bewildered and embittered; to the Christian, to the agnostic and to the atheist; it has tried to comfort the afflicted, and to challenge the comfortable.

Those who have been to Corrymeela can talk about it best. Their individual experiences are part of the whole that is Corrymeela and what it is trying to do. The story of Corrymeela is partly the story of Peg Healey and Gerry McCambridge and Harold Good.

On August 9, 1971, Desmond Healey, a Roman Catholic boy of 14 years and 8 months was shot dead by British troops in one of Belfast's Catholic housing estates. On that day there had been fierce rioting, arson and bloodshed all over the city, in the wake of an internment round-up of terrorist suspects, many of whom were innocent. Belfast was in turmoil. Desmond Healey was just another casualty in the violence.

At his inquest, the Army claimed that he had been about to throw a petrol bomb. After warnings, an order was given and he was shot once, in the chest. But another witness claimed later that Desmond Healey had been carrying only a bottle of sauce. The jury returned an open verdict. For three days Desmond's body lay unidentified. Peg Healey thought that he was staying with relatives and had not come home amid the violence and confusion. Desmond had three brothers—Ted, a twin; Michael, a younger brother who is an epileptic; and Danny, the youngest. A few months after his death, Desmond's father also died, at 42. Friends said that he never recovered from his son's death.

Peg Healey looks older than her age, in the mid-forties. She is nervous and highly strung. She has brown hair and a tired smile. Her suffering shows in her face.

I did not dare to believe that Desmond was dead. I just could not accept it at first. Then when I began to realize what had happened a terrible hatred welled up in me. My son Michael went wild. He wanted to kill all around him. I had an awful job preventing him from joining some organization. All he wanted was revenge. Give Michael a gun and he would have murdered everybody, being an epileptic, you know, he was a bundle of nerves anyway and then his brother liked him. Ted, Desmond's twin, was very quiet. Ted was quite good at school until it happened.

He was very brainy but he seemed to go down, naturally enough. With not talkin' and not eatin' and missin' school. After that there was no point in keeping Ted on. It was the school teacher that got him to see a psychiatrist. Danny, the youngest boy, he didn't say much. He was quiet, just like his father, but he felt it all the same.

I showed my hatred. Given a chance I would have killed a soldier. I even hit one with a bin lid when they came to search the house. They gave me a terrible time. Searching the house, tearing up the floor boards. They even sent me a painted bin lid as a Christmas present. They sent me a card assuring me of their attention 'at all times'. I could not think straight about that for a long time.

I could not even pass them in the street without shouting at them. When I heard on the news that soldiers had been killed I did not care how many were lying dead. I thought 'maybe that's the one that shot my child'. I didn't even care about their mothers. It was their fault for letting them come to Ireland. I just looked on the soldiers as animals. God, how I hated them.

The worst thing that happened was when someone sent Ted a Mass card. It was on the very anniversary of the other boy's death. The Mass card was for Ted. They were going to murder him. Ted was going to join his twin, and they would see to that. Terrible.

About a year after the boy's death, the Legion of Mary sent us to Corrymeela. I think Corrymeela was the first thing that brought Ted to realize that he had to live, because before that he wouldn't have gone anywhere. He just didn't seem to want to mix with anybody at all. It was the best thing that ever happened because it took him out of himself. He met people from all parts of the world. He made friends even, and he is very good with children. And Corrymeela helped him to find a steady job. Corrymeela is so homely. The housekeeper, Anna Glass, is very nice, she was good to us. And the others too.

11

It helped Michael. He really showed his brother's death. He was ready to knife the soldiers, throw stones and everything else. I didn't know what was going to happen to him. I was afraid to let him through the front door. He had this thing about Protestants, they were as bad as the Army. He would not trust anybody but Catholics. But Corrymeela did help him.

He is now at a special school in England for epileptics and he wouldn't have went otherwise because the soldiers were English, but he met so many people from all over the world at Corrymeela and this gave him a broader outlook. He realized not everybody was bad. All Protestants weren't bad and all Catholics weren't good. It meant to him that he realized he could mix and that people had feelings. Corrymeela made a terrific difference to him. I think it also helped me. I still go to Mass but I have not taken the Sacraments, except once, since the boy died. A priest in chapel said 'if you can't forgive your enemy there is no point in taking Communion'. Well, I couldn't forgive. One priest I really liked said 'God does not expect you to forgive suddenly. It will come'. He asked me if I wanted to take Communion and I did, the next morning. Later on that priest was transferred to another position and I haven't taken the Sacraments since.

One day at Corrymeela I remember coming back to my room and I found my bedclothes in tatters and my own clothes all torn. Somebody had written 'Fenian bastards'. I was ready to go home. I felt everybody was against me. The group leaders were terribly hurt. They turned over everything to find out who did it and they talked me into staying.

About four or five days later I was told who did it. It was a wee boy whose father and mother had abandoned him and he was with a bunch of orphans at Corrymeela. I realized that he was not bad, only jealous. He was jealous of Michael and Danny because they had a mother. He really was looking for a bit of love. After that he came to me every night and I took him on my knee. Maybe I learnt something from that.

It was Ray Davey, the Leader of the Corrymeela Community who made the difference about the soldiers. It was just the way he talked and listened. I'm still not too much in love with the soldiers, but I suppose you have to try hard to stop hating. I began to think about the soldiers' mothers, or their wives or children, a life is a life. Maybe some of them have been through what I have been through.

It is only lately that I stop myself from shouting at them in the street. I still don't like them, but now I turn my back on them. I don't know about this thing forgiveness. But I do know that Corrymeela helped me and it helped Danny and Michael and Ted. I don't know how it will all go in the end, but I suppose we'll have to live together no matter what way it goes...

Gerry McCambridge came to Corrymeela in 1965 during the first of the Family Weeks. He is a middle-aged family man, with eight children. An accountant by profession, he left a full-time job because of illness. He did not return to full-time practice. He accepted an invitation to become the bursar of Corrymeela on a part-time basis. He has lost out financially in doing so, but the work of Corrymeela rewards him beyond money.

Gerry McCambridge is tall, thin and intense. He is a Catholic and a deeply questioning one. His story begins in the 1920's.

We lived in a mainly Protestant part of Belfast, we were the only Catholics in the district, my mother often said that the best neighbours we ever had were Protestants. I was very young, when the 'Troubles' of the 'twenties erupted and we had to flee for our lives into a Catholic ghetto. A number of Protestant men—not our neighbours, they were strangers—burst into the house. My mother was holding me in her arms. I remember one of them holding a pistol to her head and I could see the white of the barrel ring in her flesh. My family told me afterwards that I fainted. That whole experience was dreadful.

For a long time after the incident I never stopped asking why we had to leave home. I never got an answer that satisfied me. Years later, on the day I qualified as an accountant, I was sickened when the kindly secretary of the Institute told me that it might be difficult for me to get a job in one of the Belfast offices because I was a Catholic. Strangely, however, I felt no lasting bitterness.

13

At college I had grown to know and to admire the Apostle Paul and all he had to say. I knew by heart his wonderful epistle on love. I kept asking myself 'Why do Catholics and Protestants hate each other so much? They believe in the same God, even if they worship in different ways. Surely this faith should unite them, instead of creating so much frightening enmity'.

I was also deeply concerned about the Church's teaching that there is no salvation outside Catholicism. It was by the mere accident of birth that I was not in the Protestant tradition, but was I to believe that good and God-fearing Protestants were to be denied salvation? I was deeply worried also about the Catholic teaching on mixed marriages. I felt that such rules were highly insulting to Protestants. I felt that no man and no institution had the right to interfere in such matters.

Toleration, I believe, is one of the priceless jewels of love. And when you live in a religious enclave, as we did, and your children are indoctrinated in a ghetto school it is difficult to achieve this toleration. My wife, Teresa, and I were determined that our children should have the chance to adopt a more Christian attitude towards all matters concerning Christians of other traditions. That is why we came to Corrymeela and why we brought the family with us. We wanted our children to meet Protestant children, to mix with them and to learn from them. And we thought we might learn something ourselves.

Teresa and I were both apprehensive. Neither knew quite what to expect. For the first time we met a number of Protestant ministers and we had the opportunity to talk to them in depth. It was a revealing experience. We realized that they had much the same problems with their children as we had with ours.

It was the first time too that we had attended worship outside the Catholic liturgy. We were a bit worried before the Church service began. For the first time we heard the lovely prayer of Saint Francis—'Lord make me an instrument of Thy Peace'. Then we had the Lord's Prayer, which—as the children said—was the same as 'ours', with a bit tagged on at the end. Then to my great joy the minister chose my beloved Saint Paul's words on charity as his reading, and the words took on a new meaning for all of us.

That evening my wife Teresa and I went for a walk. It was a glorious night, with the moon silver across the sea to the shores of Rathlin Island, and an air of stillness abroad. We were silent in the eloquence of such beauty. Then Teresa spoke, and as mothers do sometimes, she put a profundity of truth in a few simple words. 'These are good people', she said 'Thank God for them'. And that is what Corrymeela is trying to be about. People and their goodness.

But Corrymeela is not just a nice big house on a clifftop with a beautiful view over the sea. Corrymeela is the men and women who form the Community. It gives friendship, a true and genuine friendship, a feeling of belonging. But it makes its demands. It demands sharing, and a sense of selflessness. It preserves individuality, but that individuality becomes part of a family. There is the endless exchange of views with all kinds of people. This in Northern Ireland terms is almost revolutionary.

It was the late Sir Tyrone Guthrie, that giant of the theatre and a fine Ulsterman, who said that we were born apart, we lived apart, we prayed apart, we worked apart. We never learnt to come together and made no attempt, because there were no institutions that made it possible. Corrymeela is an effort to set that right. Corrymeela and all it stands for has helped to give me some of the answers to the questions I asked so long ago. Maybe not all the answers, but some of them.

Harold Good, the Director of the Corrymeela Centre at Ballycastle is smallish, stocky and articulate. Ordained as a Methodist minister, his widely varied clerical career took him to the Republic of Ireland, the United States, and to a working-class area in the heart of Belfast's sectarian violence, and all before forty. His path to Corrymeela was not a direct progression. It just happened that way. Harold Good has definite ideas about Christianity and the modern world. He is forthright and challenging. His working-class ministry in Northern Ireland was fraught with difficulties, in the midst of the dangers and heartbreaks of the civil war. At one point he wanted to get out of Northern Ireland to go back to America. He came to Corrymeela. He tells his own story.

My background was fairly conventional. I was born into the organized Church. My father was a minister. So is my brother. I was reared and educated within the narrowness of Northern Ireland. One of my first postings was to the Irish Republic. This pushed back the horizons a bit. Then I went to America for four years. I spent two in a team ministry in Ohio, specializing in youth work. I enrolled for two further years in a seminary in Indianapolis and worked with the Church, partly as a hospital intern, partly with emotionally disturbed children.

I came back to Ireland full of what I thought were the new ideas from America in urban ministry. My church in Belfast's Agnes Street was rough and tough. But the people were warm-hearted, and they had enormous problems, problems of redevelopment, of marriage and drink and gambling and all the kinds of problems that men and women everywhere struggle with. I was trying to get to grips with the challenge of a twentieth-century urban ministry when the Irish troubles came like a bolt from a clear sky. Once again the Irish problem erupted like a volcano of violence and we were all swept up in the smoke and the fire and the ashes.

The Agnes Street Church was in the flashpoint zone near a Catholic area. Severe rioting broke out. All night they were on the streets, with fists and bottles, and stones and boots crunching. We arrived for Church on that Sunday morning to find all the pavement stones torn up for ammunition and barricades. I have never seen anything like it in my life, apart from America and that had been on television.

So we made a snap decision to keep the Church open day and night for people to rest, or to get something to eat, or to pray for peace, or just to pray. Someone said 'you don't know what you are letting yourself in for'. And he was right. Often there were up to a hundred people in the Church at any one time. Yet it seemed the right thing to do, to keep the doors open and the lights on when all around was dark.

On one of those awful days I went round to the back of the Church and I found a group of children, some of them hardly older than five years, trying to make petrol bombs. I was aghast. Some of those kids were in my Sunday school. I was furious at the adults who led them to this. But my anger gradually turned towards the whole system that had made people behave in this way. I remember going on television and saying this. And later that broadcast caused me great anguish.

Some of my people felt I had let the side down. Here was a Protestant minister and he seemed to be condemning his own side. But I had no side. My side was the Kingdom of God, not the United Kingdom or a United Ireland. I began to realize more and more how little I and others knew about the people and their basic fears, and how little some of them knew about the real burden and the responsibility of the Christian Gospel.

During that time I was asked by several parents to appear in court to speak on behalf of their children who had been accused of theft. One of the boys was a leader in our Boys' Brigade group. He was bright, and active in the Sunday school. And that day I promised myself that, with the help of others, everything possible should be done to help the young people of the area. So we converted part of the Church hall into a youth club, we reconstructed a playground near the Church. I suppose all this involvement with people and all their everyday urban problems helped to lead me indirectly to Corrymeela. But it was not a clearly defined path.

Our Church was due to merge with another because of redevelopment and the scattering congregation, and I knew that I would be looking for a job. My wife and I had mentally committed ourselves to go to North America where a position had been offered to me. But I dithered. There were posting delays, and other delays. At heart I felt that something was holding me back. Maybe it was my conscience that would not let me desert a ship in trouble. Maybe it was something deeper. I spent some time in a different Church trying to sort out my own mind. Eventually I talked to Ray Davey. I had known Ray and had admired the Community's work. He told me that the position of Director at the Ballycastle centre was open.

I thought about it, and it seemed to make sense. A pattern seemed to be emerging. Maybe I was not led, but looking back I think I was placed. The whole point about Corrymeela is that I did not have to go there. I actually chose to go. That's what gives the whole thing its meaning.

People said to me 'have you left the ministry, or have you become the leader of a holiday camp?' It is neither.

Really it is the extension of my ministry in Belfast. But at Corrymeela there is a new atmosphere. There is a sense of personal freedom. People are free to relate to one another without feeling prevented from doing so by the barriers of religion and the burdens of tradition. It is a tremendous privilege to be able to relate to all kinds of people pastorally, people like politicians who drop in and share their anxieties, or an old woman from the backstreets of Belfast.

You get all kinds of little miracles, at least you think they are miracles, as when the wife of an IRA man and the wife of a Protestant extremist get together, they get to talk, they even share family worship. That, in our context of bitterness and hatred, is a miracle and these happen all the time.

And there is a privilege of breadth, of sharing Christianity with those from other disciplines and from other countries. You get the feeling of a universal concern which helps to lift you up in the bad days, and, believe me, there are really dark, grim, bad days. And there is the challenge of Corrymeela, of relating to people who are outside the active life of any church. What does a minister say to them, that is relevant and meaningful and which they can accept and apply to their own situation?

And there is tension within Corrymeela itself. People get the impression that a Christian community should be made up of people who hold hands, sing hymns and pretend that they have no big differences of opinion. Corrymeela is so real that we have all the tensions that exist outside. We are trying to overcome these tensions in our own way, but we recognize those tensions in ourselves. Out of those tensions, both inside and outside, we are trying to learn how to build bridges not only for others, but for one another.

Genesis

Many streams converged upon the river that became the Corrymeela project. The concept hinged around the whole idea of Christian Community. One of the main driving forces in that search for a new identity was Ray Davey.

The son of a Presbyterian minister, Ray Davey was reared in the small cosy village of Dunmurry, five miles South of Belfast. He grew up as a middle-class Protestant in the liberal and evangelical tradition of the 1930's. In Church life, personal salvation was stressed, the emphasis was on personal morality, but little was said about social morality. For the most part the Church's commitment to work, commerce and industry, and social and political structures was given little or no thought in Northern Ireland. The Gospel was interpreted in individualistic terms. Its social significance was largely unheeded.

Ray Davey conformed to the Establishment in his early days. He took a General B.A. degree at Queen's University in Belfast and studied theology at Belfast and Edinburgh. He became Assistant Minister in Bangor in 1939. He was treading the same sedate

Ray Davey

path of many of his Church contemporaries. The comfortable world of Ulster Protestantism was shattered by the outbreak of World War II.

A number of Ray Davey's friends joined the Army, though conscription was not introduced in Northern Ireland. Davey felt that his role was not to be on the sidelines, and he joined the Y.M.C.A. as a field secretary carrying out welfare work with the Army. On New Year's Day 1941 he landed in the Middle East and took part in the North African Campaign. Within 18 months he was taken prisoner by Rommel's Afrika Korps at Tobruk and he spent the rest of the war in prison camps—three in Italy and three in Germany.

In those years of hardship and deprivation, Davey's internationalism developed, as did his ideas for a new kind of Christian community. He, and others, experimented at Tobruk, in the Western Desert and in the prison camps. They met together as Christians to encourage one another and to grow to a deeper understanding of a personal faith within a community context.

After the war, Davey, then in his early thirties, wrote 'Don't Fence Me In', a best-selling book about his experiences. In this book his ideas on community work were crystallized. In 1946 he wrote 'Christian Community, in spite of all its lamentable divisions and failure, is the only hope for the world. Already it has outlived many cultures and civilizations. It has done this and will do it again because, in the last analysis, it is the only true community. All other communities, be they relatively good or bad, are transient, relative or

22

sectional, appealing to one particular age, or one section or one race. The Christian Community transcends colour and class, its terms of reference and its motive power are from beyond, outside man himself.'

But what kind of Christian Community? That was the major question facing Davey and his contemporaries. Yet Ray Davey had one distinct practical advantage. He had been appointed the first full-time Chaplain to the Presbyterian students at Queen's University. They began to develop a sense of community within the University, though loosely tied to the Church at large. Davey was an effective Chaplain. A quiet, self-effacing person, he had determination and drive, and he had the gift of being able to communicate to young people in their own terms. And a small group of students at University in the early 'sixties, partly inspired by Davey, felt that the Church was in danger of losing sight of its foundations as a Community of believers bonded by love.

In the search for a practical expression to their thinking, members of the group visited Christian communities at Iona, in Scotland; Agape in Italy; and Taizé, in France.

One of the central philosophies of the Iona Community, that God was concerned about the totality of life and not just the spiritual side, had a profound effect on the group. These ideas were expressed by George F. MacLeod (now Lord MacLeod of Fuinary), the Founder and first Leader of the Iona Community, in his book 'Only One Way Left'.

'I am recovering the claim that Jesus was not crucified in a Cathedral between two candles, but on a cross between two thieves; on the town garbage-heap; at a cross-roads so cosmopolitan that they had to write His title in Hebrew and in Latin and in Greek, (or shall we say in English, in Bantu and in Afrikaans?); at the kind of place where cynics talk smut and thieves curse, and soldiers gamble. Because that is where He died. And that is what He died about. And that is what a churchman should be and what churchmanship should be about.'

The Irish group was also influenced by Pastor Tullio Vinay and his new Youth Village of Agape, in the Italian Alps bordering on France. Vinay, a burly and dynamic Italian with deep set eyes and a winning smile, had already made a name for himself as the Waldensian Pastor at Florence. His courage and his compassion helped to save some sixty Jews from the Gestapo during the war and in that city he is still known as the 'Rabbi of Florence'.

After the war he embarked upon the Agape project declaring 'we will carve the face of Christ in the Alps'. He, and others, designed a Youth Village to express the idea of Christian unity, and established an international centre for discussion and encounter.

Then in 1962, Vinay and a number of professionally qualified young people, went to live at Riesi in the South of Sicily. Riesi is in one of the most depressed areas of Europe and it was a slum, morally and spiritually, as well as materially. Vinay and the members of Servizio Cristiano lived with the people in the midst of their hardship, their exploitation, and their poverty, and they tried to work out together the Christian message by facing the day-to-day problems of men and women whatever those problems might be. Here was a group who were deeply committed Christians, yet in no sense pietistic, or 'holier-than-thou'.

Tullio Vinay himself underlined what the Irish students had tried to find. 'We must not bring an empty message that makes little impact on our generation. We must live. We must incarnate the problems, the difficulties of men, be they hunger or unemployment in order to bring them the message of the Kingdom of Christ which is a message of reconciliation, of service and of love.'

At Taizé in the Burgundy region of France, the Irish visitors found a group of Christians who had a tremendously strong spiritual base. That strength had come partly from the re-examination of what Christianity in the modern world really involved. Men and women of all kinds, believers and non-believers, were made welcome at Taizé to share in witness of this spiritual strength. But most impressive of all, the members of the Taizé Community were trying to work out their Christian commitment in a practical sense by being involved with men and women in what they called 'the keypoints in their lives', whether that involvement took place in Chicago or Coventry, Alsace or Algeria.

Therefore, in a very practical way these different strands from the various parts of Europe began to be knit together within the fabric of Northern Ireland, and it was decided to call together a larger group of people who were known to be interested in the idea of establishing a new Christian community. Some were ministers from the Protestant Churches, most were lay men and women from widely differing backgrounds. This larger group had been meeting for several months and its members were beginning to face the realities of working out a Community. The maturity of the older men and women was intended to balance the enthusiasm of the students.

Two people were with Ray Davey when he wrote the initial letters of invitation to the first of the Corrymeela meetings. They were the Rev. John Morrow and the Rev. Alec Watson, both young Irish Presbyterian ministers and both members of the Iona Community. Another group led by Dr. Bill Breakey, a psychiatrist, had studied different Christian communities in depth, and was influential in the development of Corrymeela. From the very beginning Corrymeela had a nucleus of people who were impatient with the Church. Some were impatient with its theology, others were impatient because of the general attitude of complacency and triumphalism. All, or nearly all, were rebels, but they were rebels from within. They were critics, yet it was criticism not from the cynic but from those who cared. They were a group of Christians seeking to discover what Christian commitment meant and what it could be.

The first meeting of the group that was eventually to become the Corrymeela Community took place in the Presbyterian Centre at Queen's University in September 1964. About forty people attended. There were nearly forty different and well-articulated ideas as to what should be done. The most important decision they took was to meet again, and they met regularly for the next four months.

At Christmas they had a one-day retreat. And at the end of January 1966, the group heard that premises at Ballycastle, known as Corrymeela, were up for sale. They were owned by the Holiday Fellowship, an organization which had used the building as a site for open-air and hiking holidays. The Corrymeela group decided to begin negotiation for purchase. The cost was £6,500. It was not an exorbitant sum, but the Corrymeela members at that time had no funds whatsoever. They set themselves two weeks to raise the money and they did so by interest-free loans and gifts, and by sheer hard work. Each person gave as much as he could, and there were a number of generous and anonymous donations. One man alone gave £2,000. One member of the Community recalled that he had lunch or dinner with about twenty of the leading people in Northern Ireland who were known for their views on political reconciliation. He got virtually no response in terms of hard cash. Many of these people liked the idea, but the money came mainly from relatively unknown people who were prepared to take a risk and to back the Corrymeela idea with their money.

There was some delay about negotiations and Ray Davey became increasingly anxious as time dragged on. The Corrymeela building was an attractive property and there was always the danger of a much higher bid coming in. Finally one weekend Davey rang up the group's estate agent and suggested that he should push the owners for a definite acceptance of the offer. The estate agent did just that, and the offer was accepted. After that weekend a much higher bid was made from another quarter, but the firm kept honour-

Corrymeela

ably to its commitment and the Corrymeela building with its enormous potential and superb setting passed into the control of the new Community.

The decision to use the name Corrymeela for the centre came slowly but firmly. Its beauty and uniqueness had its own appeal. Besides, the name Corrymeela which had been used for the original building, was taken from a townland nearby, and its translation from the Gaelic meant 'The Hill of Harmony'. Such a title for such a centre was apt and irresistible.

Despite its potential, the Corrymeela building did not look inspiring. Davey and several friends travelled to Ballycastle and saw Corrymeela, high on its clifftop in the cutting bleakness of an Irish winter. The building had been painted a dull green, part of the woodwork had rotted, cattle were grazing on the lawn in front of the house, the garden was overgrown, there was no sign of life about the place. As the cold wind whistled in from the choppy water of the North Channel, the physical Corrymeela looked a forbidding prospect. There was much to be done.

However, the group took legal possession of the site in June 1965 and Corrymeela began to come to life. They had very little money, but they had something more important. They had a large group of people committed to an idea. They had something to bite on, they had a physical reality to appreciate.

The first Corrymeela Bulletin of October 1965 captured the excitement of those days. Anne Clark, who took part in one of the workcamps, wrote:

> It was with apprehension that I arrived there late one evening in July to begin what turned out to be three of the most enjoyable

29

weeks I have ever spent. My first thoughts were of the size of the building. It was enormous, yet compact and somehow stately in appearance.

Someone suspended at the top of an extended ladder was touching up a few rusty spots with red lead and a few others were packing away brushes and tins in one of the chalets.

Work in Corrymeela really was work. I doubt very much if any of us would have undertaken to dig and paint with quite so much enthusiasm and gusto had we been doing it at home. That was the peculiar thing about Corrymeela, the work just seemed to get done without us realizing that we were actually doing it. Our foreman, Billy McAlister, had the amazing ability of being able to bring the very best out of us all and making us feel that our contribution was vital.

Cooking, washing up and general household chores were shared by all, and even the routine job of washing up had very few dull moments... Morning and evening worship was conducted by campers and the varied ways in which worship was conducted made it more meaningful. Some of us considered that to be the factor which created the atmosphere and enthusiasm which few of us until then had experienced.

Even the thought of a soft bed, a bath and a fire did not stop any of us feeling sorry about leaving. We all felt we had achieved something worthwhile. In seven weeks Corrymeela had changed from dull green to brilliant white, and everyone in some measure had helped to bring about this transformation.

The policy of holding workcamps was, and still is, deliberate. Much of the life, the hope and the spirit of Corrymeela has been generated through these camps. When people come and work together a bond is created and they are able to relate to each other at a deeper level. In the normal type of conference people are often separated into the articulate and the inarticulate, but in a workcamp everyone has a part to play. There is a tremendous sense of release and people begin to feel that each can contribute, and that they really belong. At a workcamp people get to know each other, they get to trust each other, and a sense of comradeship and unity develops.

Two people in particular played a leading part. Billy McAlister, he became the general *factotum*, appeared almost from nowhere. He happened to be in the right place at the right time. Billy, then in his sixties, was a retired railway worker and a widower. He was an elder in the Presbyterian Church. He had a real personal faith and a knack of being able to relate to all kinds of people. In Irish terms he was looked on as 'a character', but as a 'character' he had very real practical talents to offer.

He knew about electricity, about painting, and plumbing and carpentry, and all the practical skills that Corrymeela needed. Ray Davey worried about who would live at Corrymeela and look after the building, once it had opened. He approached Billy McAlister, Billy had no ties. He said immediately that he was willing to go to Corrymeela. Ray Davey said later: 'I always feel that Billy was sent to us. I cannot put it any other way'.

Corrymeela also used the talents of Desney Kempston, the assistant chaplain at the Presbyterian Centre at Queen's. She had wide experience of workcamps in Europe and she was a talented organizer. Under the guidance of these two people the workcamps at Corrymeela flourished, and Corrymeela was gradually knocked into shape.

The life of Corrymeela was simple, and primitive, and hard. The building had been left without furniture, not even a chair. The Community had to start from scratch. Ray Davey got some old furniture from the former student centre at Queen's. When the new centre was built in 1962 the surplus furniture had been stored in an old farmhouse near Belfast.

Davey said: 'Looking back it was a very good thing that we did not have any furniture at the start. It meant that everything we got, all the work that we did, gave us a tremendous sense of achievement. Psychologically it was much better than having everything laid on from outside. I never regret that we started off as a poor organization. Whatever we got we had to work for it, but we got something far more than material gain from the work that was done.'

By the end of October 1965, just over a year since the project had been started in Belfast, Corrymeela was ready for its official opening. On a sharp but sunny day, October 30, 1965, the members of Corrymeela, their friends and their relatives gathered on the cliff-top site overlooking the blue sea which swayed far beneath to Rathlin Island and beyond. The guest of honour was Pastor Tullio Vinay who travelled from Sicily to perform the official opening.

It was a simple service, yet it had a subtle mixture of religion and secularism. There was no procession of robed church dignitaries, but there was a procession of nearly one hundred young people. They wore jeans and T-shirts, and they carried buckets, spades, mops and other symbols of the hard work that helped to make Corrymeela a physical reality.

The act of worship was led by Dr. Bill Breakey, the scripture readings were by Desney Kemptson, Ray Davey formally welcomed Tullio Vinay, and Billy McAlister invited him to declare the building open. In a real sense the service symbolized the contributions of those who had inspired and those who helped to build, Corrymeela. The scripture readings, from Ephesians, symbolized what Corrymeela was about.

'For He is our peace, who has made us both one, and has broken down the dividing wall of hostility.' Tullio Vinay in his broken, but effective, English gave Corrymeela its challenge.

In this moment of deep emotion for me I wish that with the help of the Living Lord this centre may become:

First: a place of preaching the New World as we see it in the person of Jesus Christ. The world needs to see this message in the real world of men. Here, living the New World together in work and in prayer, you may point it to all categories of men and push them to the same research, be they politicians, economists, sociologists, technicians, workers or students.

Second: a place of encounter and dialogue with all men; believers or unbelievers. The believers need the presence of unbelievers because they represent a criticism on our faith and life, the unbelievers need us if we have real news to bring. A member of the Italian Parliament once said to me: 'I am not religious but I am terribly attracted by Christ'.

Third: to be a question-mark to the Church everywhere in Europe so that it may review its structures and task and may be free from this instinct of preservation to hear the time of God for its mission in the world.

Fourth: more than all that, you—being together—have always open eyes and ears to understand when the Lord is passing nearby, to be ready to follow the way He shall indicate to you. As a Church we should not have an inferiority complex, not because we are or have something—but because every possibility is given to us as His instruments.

In his message of welcome, Ray Davey outlined the hope of Corrymeela:

We know that there is no cheap and easy route to unity. We cherish and respect the separate traditions of each Church, but we are convinced that there are multitudes of things that are crying out to be done together, and it is high time we got on with them.

We hope that Corrymeela will come to be known as 'the Open Village', open to all men of good will who are willing to meet each other, to learn from each other and to work together for the good of all.

33

Open also for all sorts of new ventures and experiments in fellowship, and study, and worship.

Open to all sorts of people; from industry, the professions, agriculture and commerce.

This is at least part of our vision. We know we are only at the beginning, and there is so much to be done.

There was much to be done. But on that sharp, sunny day in October 1965 the Corrymeela Community had done something. Its members had not sat on the fence of indecision until the iron had entered their souls. Corrymeela was a reality. The journey had begun.

The Eye of the Storm

Sam Goldwyn, the celebrated film director, once said that his next film would begin with an earthquake and work up to a climax. Corrymeela began a little like that.

Its first public meeting, during Easter 1966, made the main headlines and attracted widespread radio and television publicity. The Unionist Prime Minister of Northern Ireland, then Captain Terence O'Neill, delivered a major speech to an audience of Protestants and Roman Catholics at Corrymeela. He made a strong plea for better community understanding and appealed for a joint effort by both sides to build a better society. The 'Belfast Telegraph', the leading newspaper in Northern Ireland and one of the most influential in Ireland, commented: 'Through Captain O'Neill and those who organized the community conference, Corrymeela takes its place in Irish history'.

The theme 'Community 1966' was chosen deliberately by the conference organizers. The year 1966 was potentially explosive for Northern Ireland. It marked the Fiftieth anniversary of two separate events, each of them symbolic of the political and religious divide within the Province. Many Protestants looked back to July 1916 when thousands of their fellow countrymen died at the Battle of the Somme. Many Roman Catholics looked back to Easter 1916 in Dublin when a small band of Irish Republicans staged an abortive rebellion against the British. Initially the rebellion was a fiasco (printed copies of a Proclamation of the Republic were to be posted throughout Dublin but the military council had forgotten to buy glue), but when the British executed sixteen of the leaders, the revolutionaries changed almost overnight from being 'extremists' to heroes. Professor J.C. Beckett, the distinguished Irish historian noted: 'Ireland was quickly passing under the most dangerous of all tyrannies— the tyranny of the dead'.

Henceforth, as one writer noted, for many Irishmen, Easter was as much about insurrection as Resurrection.

Aware of the potential effect of these anniversaries, the Corrymeela Community decided to provide a platform to help translate their theories of reconciliation into practice. Brian Walker, the conference chairman who is now the Director of the international relief agency Oxfam, said: 'The conference will be a witness that Protestant and Roman Catholic groups can meet together to think about the common good of the community at a time when they might be expected to stay apart'.

Captain O'Neill's speech was delivered on Good Friday evening while body-guards and uniformed policemen huddled outside from the driving rain on the clifftop site at Corrymeela. O'Neill, with his nasalised drawl, his English County accent which sounded strange to the Ulster ear, and his aloof, rather shy, manner was not a communicator. But his words on that night were well received, even if they had an element of preaching to the converted. He said: '...the conference will not achieve its potential without frank speaking, and an admission of differences of principle. The avoidance of controversial issues may be comfortable, but it makes no real contribution to better understanding.' True to his word, O'Neill did not avoid the controversial interaction of religion and politics. He said: 'The Ulster community is a place in which two traditions meet—the Irish Catholic tradition and the British Protestant tradition. In India the place where two great rivers join together is often considered to have a particular sanctity—but it is also often a place of turbulence, as the currents from opposite directions swirl around each other. By and large these religious traditions have also been synonymous with political views. This correspondence of religion and politics has, in the past, created certain peculiar frictions in our public affairs, and prevented us from mounting a united effort to surmount other social and economic problems.'

He also touched on the controversial subject of separate schools for Protestant and Roman Catholic children. 'A major cause of division arises, some would say, from the *de facto* segregation of education along religious lines. This is a most delicate matter, and one must respect the firm convictions from which it springs. Many people have questioned, however, whether the maintenance of two distinct educational systems side by side is not wasteful of human and financial resources, and a major barrier to the promotion of communal understanding'.

O'Neill finished with a strong appeal: 'if we cannot be united in all things, let us at least be united in working together in a Christian spirit—to create better opportunities for our children, whether they come from the Falls Road or from Finaghy. In the enlightenment of education, in the dignity of work, in the security of home and family there are aims which all of us can pursue. As we advance to meet the promise of the future, let us shed the burdens of traditional grievances and ancient resentments. There is much we can do together. It must and—God willing—it will be done'.

The speech underlined the theme of Corrymeela, reconciliation and mutual understanding. The Prime Minister's words would have been unexceptionable in almost any other civilized and Christian country. But in Northern Ireland, which in 1966 was hardly Christian in the universal and contemporary sense of that term, such a speech by a Prime Minister created a stir. Dr. John E. Sayers, the irascible but high-minded editor of the liberalizing 'Belfast Telegraph', was delighted. He told Brian Walker in a private letter: 'What a perfect platform and how very finely the P.M. rose to the occasion... Given support (his speech) takes us a long step forward. But it also means that Corrymeela and all of you who belong to it are just starting'. Publicly the newspaper threw its considerable weight behind the speech. 'Captain O'Neill's challenge is not only to the IRA, it is to all those reactionary forces, Protestant as well as Roman Catholic in origin, which stand in the way of full and free co-operation in the name of Christianity'. The 'Irish Times', in the middle of its pre-occupation with

the 1916 commemorations in Dublin, noted that the Corrymeela conference had taken place 'to preserve the good relationships which have grown rapidly in recent years' in the North.

Cardinal William Conway, the head of the Roman Catholic Church in Ireland, welcomed the O'Neill speech, but in equivocal language in which he displayed the prickly sensitivity of the Irish hierarchy, he said: 'I welcome very much the appeal for goodwill and Christian charity, and I respect the sincerity with which it was made. I am bound to say, however, that I find this continuing pressure on Catholic schools, by the head of the Government very surprising and, indeed, disquieting.' Even the Corrymeela Bulletin itself reflected the air of hope that O'Neill's statement had generated. It stated: 'Northern Ireland's self-inflicted wounds are showing signs of healing... The Prime Minister's brave opening speech will be remembered not so much for its content as for the fact that it was made'.

Yet within a short time tragedy crowded out all those hopes. Only three years after the Corrymeela conference, the mobs and the marchers were out on Ulster's streets, the gun had returned to Irish politics and with it the explosions, the assassination squads, the intimidators, the murderers and the murdered, the guilty and the innocent. Within nine years, more than one thousand people had died, countless numbers had been injured, and millions of pounds of damage had been caused. Northern Ireland had descended into the whirlpool of violence that caused more casualties, more suffering and more misery than any other conflict in Ireland since the beginning of the century, and that included the Irish War of Independence.

Why were all the hopes of Corrymeela and elsewhere overtaken so swiftly by the violence?

Subsequent events showed that in 1966 liberals were miscalculating the ground swell for moderation in the Ulster community. The IRA had indeed abandoned its latest campaign in 1962 with nothing to show for its military policy except several policemen killed, over thirty people injured and damage estimated at £1,000,000. There were superficial signs that Catholics and Protestants were learning to live as neighbours. This spirit was cemented by a series of Community Weeks sponsored by the O'Neill Government. The Prime Minister of Northern Ireland had met the Prime Minister of the Republic, Sean Lemass, in a formal encounter at Stormont, the seat of the Ulster Unionist Government. Relationships on all sides seemed to be improving, even if occasional riots as in Belfast in 1964, or petrol bombs again in Belfast in 1966, were present-day reminders of a violent past.

The good signs were there but they masked an awesome legacy of bitterness, hatred and mistrust that lurked beneath the surface. For many Irishmen, the fifty years since 1916 were too short to forgive or forget.

When the British began to withdraw from Southern Ireland in 1922, six years after the Easter Rising, the 'Irish Question' was by no means settled. The problem of Irish nationhood and of Ulster's special identity and allegiance was merely postponed to plague succeeding generations. The 1920 Government of Ireland Act provided for two Irish Parliaments: one in Dublin and the other in Belfast. The Act also provided for an

All-Ireland Parliament but this was never formed. The Unionists in the North accepted part of the terms of the Act, for it ensured that the Province would remain within the United Kingdom.

The British proposals were rejected by Dublin politicians and the struggle continued. After further bitter fighting, a truce was arranged and an agreement was signed one year later on the formation of an 'Irish Free State'. This agreement in turn was totally rejected by another section of Irishmen, and civil war between the 'Free Staters' and the 'Republicans' broke out. The Free State Government showed great ruthlessness in dealing with its opponents, indeed a greater ruthlessness than the British had shown, and Republican resistance was overcome. The Irish Free State, the forerunner of today's Irish Republic, was conceived in war and established by force of arms.

The uneasy peace that began to settle over Ireland was due more to exhaustion than to a carefully prepared plan to bring a lasting solution to the whole island. The Ulster Unionists formed their own Government and Ireland became partitioned. Part of the earlier British intention was that the two parts of Ireland should co-operate under one Irish Parliament. Instead, Northern Ireland and the Republic glared at one another across the Border and remained frozen in their respective versions of a common history.

This division was mirrored within the society of Northern Ireland itself. Over one million Protestants looked to Britain for their social and cultural links. The Protestants controlled the Parliament, and by carefully institutionalized discrimination they ensured that power remained in Protestant hands. In Londonderry, for example, the local Council was ruled by a Protestant majority even though Protestants were outnumbered two to one by Roman Catholics in that city. The half million Roman Catholics in Northern Ireland, denied any meaningful role in Northern affairs, looked to Dublin and had historic and cultural links with the Republic. Protestants, in turn, argued that Catholics could not expect a significant role in Government if their allegiance lay outside Northern Ireland. Of course there were exceptions. There were Protestant Republicans and Catholic Unionists, but in general the divide in the island of Ireland was reflected in the division within Ulster itself.

Religious allegiance was the nominal distinction between the two communities. In fact there were two Nations, with two different cultures and a distinct set of values. Protestants and Catholics were not merely different brands of Christians, they were regarded by one another as different peoples. Protestants and Catholics were brought up to believe in different versions of a joint history, to admire different heroes, to hate different villains, to appreciate different flags and National songs, even to play different games.

The immense tragedy was that in all of those arid years, nothing was done of significance to bridge the gap. The Governments North and South failed ignominiously. The Churches, both Protestant and Roman Catholic, failed repeatedly to convey the basic message that true Christianity transcends all national and social barriers. Catholicism remained identified with Irish Nationalism, Protestantism remained the prisoner of Unionism. Both major Churches were content to preach about the 'love of God' on a Sunday and during

43

the rest of the week to allow Protestants and Catholics to grapple on their own with the problems of social and political morality. Tony Spencer, a sociologist from Queen's University, Belfast, claimed many years later, when the ecclesiastical rot had set in, that most Protestants, like most Catholics, had been quite unaware how their actions and those of their parents and grandparents had secularized Christianity in Ireland. 'They desecrate daily in good conscience', he said.

Yet, despite the bitter legacy of the past, Terence O'Neill on that night in Corrymeela in 1966—and many other moderates like him—looked for a light at the end of the tunnel. They were, and many still are, men and women of vision; and in 1966 there were hopeful signs for anyone who wanted to see them. But the weight of history bore down heavily on those who were trying to carry Northern Ireland into a new age.

Even as he stood at Corrymeela, O'Neill carried within him the seeds of his own destruction. An influential and ultimately powerful right-wing group in his Unionist Party bitterly resented his meeting with Sean Lemass, the Eire Premier, in 1965. O'Neill had been careful to stress that constitutional or political issues had not been discussed, but in a warning gesture that was unmistakable, the Unionist Party asked him to take no similar actions in future on his own initiative without prior consultation.

O'Neill had a concept of what a peaceful and integrated Northern Ireland might be with Roman Catholics and Protestants living in harmony, but while he gave a lead to middle-class opinion, both Roman Catholic and Protestant, his message did not seep through to enough of the working-class Protestants, whose votes ultimately dictated where the real power lay. O'Neill was a courageous Prime Minister. He was not a leader. Ultimately he did not bring enough of the people who mattered with him. Just three years after his Corrymeela speech he retired from active politics, a bitter and disillusioned man.

The demise of O'Neill and of moderate Unionism was partly due to the rise of the Rev. Ian Paisley, a fractious and loud-mouthed self-made preacher who had the ability to articulate the often unspoken fears of the Protestant majority. While O'Neill was speaking about peace and moderation at Corrymeela, Paisley in his thickly articulated Ulster accent was thanking God 'that the 1916 rebellion was a failure and that Ulster is still free from Papal tyranny'. At the beginning, Paisley was treated by some sections of the media as something of a joke. He was broad, brash and colourful; he was a man with the telling quote; his craggy countenance was a cartoonist's dream; his earlier public appearances were slightly ridiculous anti-ecumenical protests. He appeared to be a relatively unimportant crank.

But with time, Paisley emerged as a determined opponent of moderate bridge building and as an orator and a ruthless politician who could play upon the fears of many Protestants who really believed that any gesture towards Catholics or towards the Republic would lead to the Papal domination of Northern Ireland. Equally important, Paisley could mobilize these people into a cohesive and a formidable opposition, Paisley and Paisleyism became one of the most divisive forces in Ulster society at a time Ulster so badly need reconciliation. The moderates in 1966 were aware of the destructive potential of Paisley but they felt that moderation would prevail. For example in 1967 a National Opinion Poll survey showed that 90% of people would choose O'Neill in preference to Paisley to lead the country. In 1968 a Dublin newspaper, the 'Sunday Independent' chose O'Neill as their 'Man of the Year'. But in the end, Paisley won the day. A major factor in the defeat of O'Neillism was the bitter truth that O'Neill arrived politically at least a generation too late. He tried to break the log-jam of bigotry, but he did not have enough support within his party or within the country to translate his words of conciliation into action. Early in 1968 in an important television appearance he reviewed his first five years as Premier. He said that he thought the majority of Catholics appreciated that improvements had been made. But in a most significant comment, Eddie McAteer, the leader of the Nationalist Party, said that while it was true there had been talk of change, nothing had been done to take up that talk.

The potential for upheaval had been present since the 'twenties but by the mid-sixties a further dimension had been added. A new generation of articulate and politically-conscious young people, most of them Roman Catholics and many of them University trained, had become impatient with the lack of Government action to deal with the basic abuses in Ulster society. A Civil Rights Association was formed and its fire was fuelled by the kind of injustice brought to public notice by Austin Currie, a young Nationalist MP from County Tyrone.

In the village of Caledon, Currie occupied a house that had been allocated by the local Council to a young unmarried Protestant girl, even though Catholic families who had occupied other houses in Caledon had been evicted. Currie himself was removed from the house by the Police but the newspapers and radio and television reported the story widely. Northern Ireland was thrust into the national headlines and that kind of publicity was disastrous for a Government which was trying to present a picture of improving community relations as part of an attempt to bring new industries to the Province. The Civil Rights issue exploded into international prominence when the marchers were batoned, and drenched by water cannons, by the Police in Londonderry on October 5, 1968, again in full view of the press and the television cameras. From that moment, the Northern Ireland story was constantly in the world's headlines.

For the next seven years, events in Ulster unfolded with the inevitability of a Greek tragedy. The Civil Rights supporters continued their demonstrations, this led to Protestant counter-demonstrations. At the beginning there were Protestants who supported the Civil Rights Movement. But there were many more Protestants who looked on Civil Rights as a 'front' for the IRA. And there were Protestants, who could not have been called extremists at the beginning, who resented bitterly the Civil Rights claim that Catholics had been treated as 'Second-class citizens'. As the demonstrations continued the O'Neill Government hastily announced a five-point reform plan, promising among other things a fair system of house allocation and the appointment of an *Ombudsman*. O'Neill made a dramatic television broadcast and he told people bluntly that Ulster was at the cross-roads. 'What kind of Ulster do you want?' he asked. The next few months provided the answer. The reforms did not bring the marchers off the streets. On the contrary they released pent-up feelings, and the Civil Rights Movement gained further momentum. The opposition of Protestants intensified, and opinion—even in the middle ground—began to harden. O'Neill's support withered away and he resigned in April 1969.

Political instability continued and the Unionist Government gradually lost control. After prolonged rioting in Derry in 1969, and fierce sectarian warfare in Belfast during which Catholic homes were burnt to the ground by Protestants and several people, including a boy of nine, were shot dead, the British Army was called in to keep the peace. This was one of the turning points. The British Army had been in Ulster already in garrison strength, but the intervention of the Army on the streets in Belfast and Derry committed the Labour Government of Harold Wilson, and subsequent Governments, to a direct involvement in Northern Ireland affairs. It marked the beginning of a painful period in which Northern Ireland became one of the running sores of British politics. It also led indirectly to an urban guerilla war which was one of the most ferocious in Europe since World War II.

The enemy consisted mainly, though not exclusively, of the Provisional IRA which had formed itself with astonishing rapidity particularly when the Catholic areas of Belfast were seen to be defenceless against the onslaughts of Protestant extremists. The Provisional IRA, a group of ruthless militants, came into existence in 1970 after a split with the main IRA

movement which, in the years preceding the latest Troubles, had followed on a mainly political policy. The Provisional IRA embarked on a campaign which was to terrorize all the people in both communities. The campaign was dedicated to the violent expulsion of the British from Ireland once and for all, and repeated bombings, shootings and violence in general brought the years of terror, atrocity and counter-atrocity to Northern Ireland. The rise of the IRA led in turn to the creation of paramilitary Protestant forces, who also cast their shadow of violence over the whole community.

In 1971 the Unionist Government of Brian Faulkner in a last desperate gamble introduced imprisonment without trial. This made things worse, partly because at the start it was a one-sided weapon used against Catholics, and as such it acted as a recruiting agent for the Provisional IRA. The vicious fighting continued and in 1972 the British Government suspended the Northern Ireland Parliament and set about the tortuous business of trying to establish a consensus of opinion between the two communities. Despite continuing violence the British Government seemed to have achieved the impossible when politicians representing Protestants and Catholics agreed to work together in a joint administration from January 1974. However, and significantly, the hardline Protestants confirmed that they would not work with Catholics whose ultimate aim was a United Ireland. The Northern Ireland Executive, after a brave but brief attempt at shared Government across the sectarian divide, collapsed in the chaos of a prolonged national strike. This was organized and maintained by Protestants who firmly believed that a power-sharing Government was the first step to eventual domination by the Irish Republic. So once again the search for a solution began.

Behind the attempts to achieve a political settlement lay a story of the most savage urban guerilla warfare. In over six years, terrorists on both sides, Protestants and Catholics, used 244,553 lb of explosives. This was in an area smaller than Yorkshire in England. In Northern Ireland 935 civilians died; 284 soldiers died; 65 policemen died; a total of 1,284 people died. The British Government paid over £135,000,000 in compensation for damage to individuals and to property. In the middle of March 1975 another £62,000,000 in claims was outstanding.

Statistically the number of casualties might appear small in an international context. Over 1,000 people dead in Northern Ireland seemed insignificant compared to 500,000 killed in Indonesia or the 800,000 in Vietnam. Yet the Irish figure was big enough to be important and small enough to retain a perspective of human suffering. John Hume, a former Civil Rights leader—he was one of the first Catholics to hold Ministerial office in a Northern Ireland Administration—addressed Congressional leaders, Senators and Congressmen in Washington on April 25, 1974. He referred to the deaths in Ulster and said, 'the equivalent proportion to the population of the USA would be a deathrate of 150,000 people in four years of civil strife'.

The degree of violence in Northern Ireland was horrifying. Restaurants, public houses, bus stations and private dwellings were blasted without warning, or with warnings that came too late. Civilians lost limbs and eyes and minds; soldiers and police, and terrorists on both sides were killed with almost monotonous regularity. In Ulster life and death became utterly cheap.

The violence spread outside Northern Ireland. In one day alone in 1974, bombs exploded in Dublin and in Monaghan, on the Irish border, which led to the deaths of over thirty people. In Birmingham later in the year two bombs killed twenty-one people in one night. The search for a consensus in Ulster became even more urgent.

The Ulster story remained complex to the outside world. Outsiders could not understand easily why people in a nominally Christian country were tearing it and each other apart in a war which seemed to have more relation to the seventeenth century than to the twentieth. Yet stripped of all its complexities, the struggle inside Ulster was a struggle for identity. It was that same struggle that had been postponed by the Irish settlement in the 'twenties. The two nations within Ulster, the two peoples, the two communities were still there, but with one significant difference— the attempts to find agreement became more and more difficult as the violence continued.

Against this background of ignorance, prejudice, bigotry and overwhelming violence, the physical Corrymeela seemed small indeed. At first the members of the Community appeared to some observers to be merely well-meaning amateurs who are using buckets of water to try to put out a raging forest fire. The point about Corrymeela was that while the fire raged the supply of water, though small at the beginning, did not dry up.

The physical Corrymeela was limited, but the philosophy of Corrymeela had the widest implications. It was this philosophy that sustained the movement, and that attracted more and more newcomers. Corrymeela never claimed that it had all the answers. In fact the pressure was so great in the middle of the civil conflict that there was not time to make grandiose claims of any kind.

Yet the philosophies of Corrymeela, whether they had the name of Corrymeela or not, were relevant to the practical situation. The need for openness, for trust, for mutual recognition and for reconciliation was self-evident. It was precisely because those qualities had been so absent from the basic institutions of Church and State in Ireland that the explosion, when it came, was so shattering. Previous generations of Irishmen had failed. Corrymeela itself partly grew out of that failure and in its early days there was no guarantee of its success. A reconciliation centre had been established in relative peace and within an alarmingly short time it found itself caught up in a civil war. A candle flickering in the dark was threatened by the hurricane of a political upheaval which threatened to snuff it out.

But there could be no second thoughts and no easy options. For the Corrymeela Community there could be no turning back once the first steps had been taken. In the middle of the holocaust a Corrymeela Communique of 1972 showed why there could be no turning back, even if the way ahead offered neither safety nor certainty. It stated:

Very often we are asked these days if we do not feel despondent and want to give up our Corrymeela work. Of course we all do feel depressed at times, but as to giving up or giving in—we can never contemplate that. It is all too easy to become emotional and despairing at such a time. But that is no answer—in fact this is what the champions of all our violence hope for, as this is a war of nerves, a struggle between the way of naked violence and worse—when we think of recent outrages against human personality—and the way of reason, open discussion and reconciliation.

We must realize that the gunmen have their problems too, once the shootings and the bombings cease. As support for them diminishes, they know that they are finished. It is this we must work for at such a time. If it is to happen, then we must all use our influence by word and deed to support those who are intimidated, and give them courage to stand for the better way.

We in Corrymeela must be more courageous and unwearying in seeking new ways of understanding and new formulae for communal co-operation. The qualities supremely needed now are patience, courage, imagination and hope.

In Action

The story of Corrymeela in action is illustrated by a boy nicknamed 'Boxer'. He is a sturdy, high-spirited teenager with a sense of devilment and a nose for adventure that can take him towards leadership, or trouble.

Boxer is the typical modern boy who wears his youth like a badge. His hair is close-cropped in the fashion of the British 'skinheads'. He wears denim jeans, a T-shirt and white plimsolls. Boxer in full flight is undistinguishable from dozens of other teenagers who flit in and out of the headlines when football riots, or race riots, or just 'plain' riots are in the news.

Boxer lives in a tough, working-class area of Belfast. In the long rabbit-warrens of red-brick streets where the sun seldom seems to pierce the grime, the boredom is claustrophobic. There are few green playing fields, or picturesque rivers or wide open spaces where healthy young people can dissipate their excess energy. So Boxer, and many boys like him, work off their youthful zeal by stoning the British troops who venture into their area on patrol.

In the old days when there were no British troops on patrol, boys could stone the local policeman and run 'like blazes' to safety. Or they could stone each other. But British troops were beyond an adolescent's wildest dreams. Not only were they the 'old enemies' of Ireland in a predominantly Irish Republican district, they actually dressed, spoke and acted like the enemy.

And everybody knew that they could not hit back. They might, if they were taunted beyond endurance, throw a couple of tear-gas canisters. But they would not shoot children throwing stones. Children and adolescents carrying guns were a more dangerous proposition. But not stones. Boxer and his friends thought they were living dangerously.

Then Boxer came to Corrymeela. Nothing spectacular happened to him. There were no overnight transformations, no elaborate explanations, and no embarrased confessions. Boxer was just another teenager and he was treated as such, though the Corrymeela staff noticed his zest, his confidence and his innate quality of leadership. They wondered if this quality would ever be channelled in the right direction, back in his home environment.

Boxer returned home. The next day his friends Sean and Michael and Brendan knocked on his front door.

> 'You comin' out Boxer?' they asked breathlessly. 'There's a patrol of "Brits" movin' down the street. We got a few stones to bounce off their skulls. Let's see how tough the buggers are.'
>
> Boxer remained silent. He looked more than a little embarrassed.
>
> 'Wassamatter Boxer, you gettin' scared?' they asked with a note of amazement.
>
> 'No, but ... it's like this', said Boxer, with the heavy sigh of a young man who had weighed up the odds carefully. 'If I stone the "Brits" ... I won't be allowed back to Corrymeela again.'

Corrymeela does that kind of thing to some people. And it happens almost unconsciously. There is no preaching or sermonizing or slickly-presented philosophy. Corrymeela tries to speak for itself. Perhaps one of the reasons why it speaks and has spoken eloquently, yet quietly, to all sorts of people is its basic foundation. And that foundation is its interpretation of Christianity. The theory and the practice of Corrymeela are totally inter-related.

The point was underlined with clarity during a re-dedication service in 1975. Ray Davey, the Leader, said: 'We are not a social welfare body, nor a Community Relations project, nor a Community Development team, nor is this place a Conference House or a Holiday Centre. We are above all else a group of Christians who are trying to follow Christ and to do what he wants done in our society. We are disciples and therefore we accept the discipline of Christ'.

The same philosophy is put precisely by the Apostle James, the crispest of writers: 'For as the body apart from the spirit is dead, so faith apart from works is dead'.

Thus, although Corrymeela is well known for its youth work and its activities during the worst of the Irish troubles, it covers the widest spectrum of human relationships where reconciliation is needed. In all the analyses that are continuing, there is a danger—as Martin Luther King once said—of 'analysis paralysis'. There is a temptation for people and communities to become too analytical.

In the real-life situation there is no departmentalism. People experience life as a whole. They are not exclusively political or economic or religious. All these intermingle and react, one on another. Very often direct political action is not the first priority, but rather a recognition of all the aspects that make up a person's total life.

So at Corrymeela there have been, and are, many different programmes. There is the social need, based on families, individuals under stress, old people and the handicapped. There is community relations, featuring mixed groups, families, conferences and schools. There is training and leadership, with summer projects and work camps and students of all kinds. There is dialogue, with ecumenical gatherings, political-sociological conferences and any encounter situation where communication can be fostered between differing groups and individuals. It is a mistake to think that Corrymeela is merely a holiday centre or a retreat from war, though that mistake is often made. Corrymeela is a place, but it is also an attitude of mind. One of the last signs the visitor reads on his way out is the simple message 'Corrymeela begins when you go home'.

Corrymeela itself had started encouragingly, in its own home. Not only had Tullio Vinay come from Sicily to open the centre, but also the Prime Minister of Northern Ireland had given the key address at its first conference. But when the tumult had died down and the Captains and the Kings had departed, Corrymeela was left in the cool grey of subsequent weeks to try to match the words with the deeds. There were the dreams and the visions, but the routine work of each day had to be done. The building itself was only a shell. Indeed the carpet had arrived only one hour before the first conference began. It was exciting, but it was primitive. A great deal of hard work had still to be done.

It is important to remember that, from the start, the Corrymeela Community had twin focal points. The Ballycastle building on the North Antrim coast was the shop window. It kindled the imagination, but the organization, the planning and the recruitment centred on Belfast. That liaison has continued since, and it is vital to the whole concept of Corrymeela. Otherwise the Community could justifiably be accused of establishing an Irish 'Shangri-la' on the beautiful but remote North Antrim coast, while the real work—the messy and dirty work—waited to be done elsewhere.

There were still several years before the Irish troubles exploded into further violence. In these years priority was given to reconstructing the old building and to raising money. The Community organized Open Days, Autumn and Spring Fairs, covenant schemes, and its members spoke at multitudes of meetings. Corrymeela received no grants from Church or State, though later a Government Ministry did provide some financial help. Certain individuals were generous, but in the majority of cases, Corrymeela had yet to prove itself to people.

One of the first considerations was the basis of membership. Initially the members were Protestants, but they wanted to be fully representative of all the churches. Some wanted to move slowly; others wanted the Community opened up as quickly as possible. Eventually they all agreed that if their work was to be effective they needed to be open at every level to all Christians.

There were long debates about the theological basis of membership. After much discussion this was resolved simply. 'We believe in God as revealed in Jesus Christ and in the continuing work of the Holy Spirit.' The members felt that on this basis their theology would develop as they went along. Strict rigidity, it was felt, would be counter-productive. Despite its limitations and its mistakes, Corrymeela learned one basic lesson—to be flexible in order to respond to new situations and events.

This was increasingly relevant when violence exploded all over Ulster in a bloodlust of killing and revenge. A great number of people—Protestants, Catholics, agnostics, atheists—were under enormous pressure and some were in danger of their lives, particularly in Belfast.

Could Corrymeela continue merely with its discussions, its retreats and its community concept? There seemed little point in having endless debates in Ballycastle, when the real and urgent needs of Belfast and other parts of the Province were on the doorstep. In the middle of the fighting and the killing and the rioting, Ray Davey, who by 1969 was the full-time Leader of Corrymeela, decided to take the initiative. He went right into the heart of the Belfast housing estates that were locked in deep enmity one with another. On one side was a Protestant estate flying a Union Jack defiantly and chanting about its loyalty to Queen and Ulster. On the other side, across the road, were Catholics erecting barricades with stolen cars, lorries and anything they could get their hands on to protect their area from potential assassins and petrol bombers.

Throughout the troubles, neither side was blameless. Murder, arson, robbery and intimidation were committed by people from both sides of the sectarian divide.

Ray Davey, during his visit to the housing estates, discovered how Corrymeela could make a valuable contribution. The local people were worried about the effects of the violence on teenagers, and Davey and others arranged a week's holiday for them at Ballycastle.

About fifty boys and girls took part. The week was a success. Few of the children had seen the sea before and there were shrieks of excitement when they were driven down to the shore at Ballycastle on one of those days when there is a full tide and the waves tumble and cascade onto the golden ribbon of sand. There were informal discussions, and improvised concerts and barbecues.

Whatever the week meant to the children, the Corrymeela Community learnt a lot. It was the beginning of a new way of service that was meant to be relevant in a practical way. That need was underlined unconsciously by Deirdre, a shy little girl of eleven, who had seen some of the worst fighting in Belfast. She said: 'I like Corrymeela and Ballycastle. I saw a lot of shops and none of them were burnt out'.

There was a sequel to the group's stay in Ballycastle. When they returned to Belfast there was severe flooding, and many homes were damaged by filthy floodwater. So the group of children kept together, they decided to help and they worked at moving furniture and drying carpets. One woman whose house had been badly damaged said it had been worth even the flooding to experience such kindness from the young people. 'It's all right, Missus', said one of the boys, 'we've been to Corrymeela'.

It was the young people in particular who seemed to be able to relate to the atmosphere of Corrymeela. Kathleen Davey, the wife of the Leader, tells a story about the day she was gardening in the front of Corrymeela House when the minibus ground to a halt outside and disgorged its motley crew of young boys from one of the more dismal and violent parts of Belfast. Immediately the boys clambered to the top of a nearby chalet which they used as a vantage point for a mock 'machine-gun' attack, which was all too real in the streets where they lived.

Kathleen Davey worked quietly at the bed of marigold flowers. Eventually the boys tired of their mock battle. They wandered over. After a long pause one boy pointed to the marigolds and said: 'My God, them's lovely'.

After that, they worked each day with Kathleen Davey at the flowers. At the end of their visit she gave each of them a marigold. Off they went in the bus, each of them clasping a marigold to his bosom.

Three weeks later, Kathleen Davey received a letter. It read: 'My marigold has died. Can I come back to Corrymeela...?' It was signed 'With love, Your little Gardener'.

One of the most dramatic periods in Corrymeela's history was the evacuation of large numbers of children from Belfast during the Internment crisis in August 1971. Troops and police rounded up scores of people suspected of terrorist activities. Many of these people were utterly innocent. Some three hundred men were taken in a series of dawn raids from Roman Catholic areas when troops burst into their homes and carried them away. Though Internment had been a possibility for some time, the immediate reaction was explosive.

Within twenty-four hours some fourteen people had been killed. There was fierce rioting, widespread arson and a degree of looting. Street lamps and pavement stones were torn up to make barricades; lorries and cars were hi-jacked. In twenty-four hours firemen dealt with fifty-seven fires. At another thirty-five they were prevented from getting close to the blaze by rioting mobs. Dozens of terrace houses were set on fire. A heavy blanket of fear settled over Belfast. It was almost as visible as the black pall of smoke that hung over the city.

Many of the children from the worst affected areas needed help. And Corrymeela became directly involved. Liz Maxwell, a Corrymeela worker in one of the flashpoint areas, sent an S.O.S. to Ballycastle. Immediately, Corrymeela decided to evacuate the children. Within hours they had been given permission to billet the children in local schools, which were empty at that period of school holidays. Bureaucracy was minimized. Red tape was cut at speed. One headmaster said: 'Really we should have the Committee's permission to do this, but you have not time. Here, take the keys'.

The major problem was to evacuate the children in safety. Some of the Corrymeela workers tried to drive their minibus to the area of the worst fighting. The police and army said it was dangerous to go any further. The Corrymeela workers kept in touch with Liz Maxwell by 'phone. The main roads were blocked by barricades. Suddenly three local girls appeared almost miraculously, clambouring out of a hedge. They had come 'cross-country' to guide the bus in. They found one partially-completed barricade. The barricade builders looked covetously at the minibus. The young girls told them in no uncertain manner where to get off. At the roadside, men stood with automatic rifles at the ready. Eventually they decided to let the bus through. An effective route was established from the heart of the troubled areas and about three hundred children in all were evacuated.

The relief operation lasted some two weeks. Kathleen Davey and her helpers had to learn how to cater in school canteens for large numbers—and quickly. They learnt—and quickly. It was a most difficult time. Some children were very young and missed their parents. Some older children wanted to get back to Belfast, despite the fighting. One batch of teenagers set off to walk the fifty-five miles on foot. In desperation, the Corrymeela helpers headed them off and asked them what they would like to do. They said they would like to see the Coleraine football ground. Corrymeela contacted the Coleraine Manager, Bertie Peacock, an ex-Irish international and Glasgow Celtic player. Peacock sized up the situation quickly. He agreed to help and gave the teenagers the VIP treatment. They were happy. Afterwards they went back again to Corrymeela. All kinds of people made their contributions in those difficult and dangerous days.

This relief work did much to establish Corrymeela within the Ballycastle community. The purpose of Corrymeela was made visible in the streets of the town. They saw the children of the city and the state they were in. The response was immediate and inspiring. Many people flocked to Corrymeela and asked if they could help. The Ballycastle Community Association organized a house-to-house collection and some £600 was given to Corrymeela for its work. Corrymeela started to become part of the local scenery. It was being accepted at all levels.

But this venture had a chain reaction. It became clear that Corrymeela had to expand physically. This led to the financing and building of the Tara Village—a new unit of chalets, with kitchen and washing facilities and a common room. This is now used all the year round, and for all sorts of youth groups.

The chain reaction went further. The Corrymeela workers soon realized that it was pointless to have young people for occasional weekends and then to forget about them once they had gone to their homes. It was essential to maintain the spirit of Corrymeela in Belfast and Derry and elsewhere. The obvious answer was to establish groups in these places. And this has been continuing for several years.

Corrymeela itself has four groups and it works closely with a number of others. Each group has developed a programme of its own and it meets each week. Apart from weekend visits to Corrymeela every month, they go further afield to England, Wales and to the Irish Republic. Billy, a tough Protestant boy from one of the groups, said recently: 'This has given me a new lease of life. If I was not here, I would be out on the streets, and you know what that means'.

One important aspect of youth work at Corrymeela has been the 'twinnings' where a Catholic and a Protestant school organize a field week or a weekend together. Corrymeela is ideal for this kind of programme, as it is in the middle of one of the most celebrated geological areas in the British Isles. And as Corrymeela has often pointed out, there is no Protestant and no Catholic geology, just geology.

Many schools have taken up such projects and in their common concern for geology or geography, they have found a new respect and understanding for one another. Children who might not have met a Protestant or a Catholic during their entire school career can meet at Corrymeela and on equal terms. One of the most revealing stories concerns Jimmy, a boy who took part in a mixed-school project. When he came back to Belfast he asked if he could return to Corrymeela, but with the same mixed group of children. He explained why. 'At first I was a bit scared to go off, as I knew there might be fighting. I was told that you could get a "good kicking" from the other side. But we found out that the other boys were just like us and we liked them'.

Mary, a polite little girl in the same party, wrote to Corrymeela to say: 'Thank you'. She ended her letter: 'It really was a wonderful time. I changed my attitude to teachers, and to Protestants'. Reconciliation was seeping through at the most unexpected levels...

The different strands of youth work come to a climax each summer at Corrymeela and beyond. The many projects include holidays for handicapped and sub-normal children, for small groups of special-care Protestant and Catholic children, and joint projects in the cities. A large number of volunteers are always needed to maintain and organize these activities, and Corrymeela depends greatly on young people from home and abroad. The quality of Corrymeela work depends on the calibre and the caring of the helpers, and with some exceptions they have been of a high standard.

During the Internment crisis, for example, some sixty helpers appeared as if from nowhere. They, and the others, helped to make a rocky path much more smooth.

One by-product of inestimable significance is the number of young people who are inspired by their experience at Corrymeela to take up community and youth work on a full-time and professional basis. A number of people who gained their first experience at Corrymeela now hold key posts in teaching and administration. There are others, of course, who come to Corrymeela, pass through, and pass on. But when the penny drops, there can be a rich reward.

Such youth work is vital, but Corrymeela is much more than a youth camp. The Community's response has been to relate to needs and situations and not only to age groups.

For example, Corrymeela has established the 'Family Weeks' during which women and children, Catholics and Protestants, can find rest away from the areas of tension. These groups have included the family of an IRA officer shot dead by British troops, the family of Protestant paramilitary men, the family of other Republicans and Loyalists, and families of no strong political or religious persuasion who were simply caught in the line of fire.

It is difficult to exaggerate the tension and the pressure under which families in the troubled areas have been living. One mother at Corrymeela told how she made her two young sons change into their pyjamas every day directly after they came home from school. That way, they would not be tempted to go outside and therefore risk becoming involved in the violence. And this went on for month after month after month.

But in the peace and the beauty of Corrymeela the families could relax and discuss—with one another—their deepest fears and anxieties. Attitudes changed and in some cases this change persisted long after the people had left Corrymeela. During one week, two hardline families from opposing areas came with fixed views. They confessed that they had never been able to talk in the same way. Both families are keeping in touch today.

Another group suffered during the violence. It was the old. Many live alone and many have been victims of rumour and fear. Every week in the summer, Corrymeela organizes joint holidays for these people. Here again the barriers are softened or broken down.

'Old Johnny' from a hardline Protestant area became very friendly with a nun from the United States. Johnny did not know she was a Catholic nun. At the end of his visit a friend said: 'Johnny, you were very friendly with that wee nun'.

'Oh, you are wrong', said Johnny, 'she is not a nun. She is wearing the uniform of a district nurse'. Johnny's background had not let him admit to being friendly with 'the other side', but perhaps he never quite looked at nuns in the same way again. One old-age pensioner underlined the barrenness of all the wasted years when he said: 'If we had had places like this fifty years ago, we would not have any of these troubles today'.

Corrymeela became a retreat for the worried, the weary and the wrecked, some of them had been physically tortured. One man had been worked over systematically with a razor. Corrymeela did not ask questions, for there would have been no answers. But the door was, and is, always open. The hard men, and the weak men, on both sides know that.

In all of these Family Weeks a very real distinction emerged between religion, which to many was another word for sectarianism, and Christianity, which began to mean something different. One little girl confided to a lady helper: 'My Mummy knows what is wrong with this country. It's them Protestants'.

The lady took a deep breath and said: 'Well, I'm a Protestant'.

The little girl said: 'But ah, you are not a Protestant when you are at Corrymeela'. The same distinction was made in a different way by Martha, a Protestant grandmother of ten, who in her own inarticulate way led a simple communal prayer. She asked God's blessing on all children. And she said: 'Four of my own grandchildren are Catholics, and I love them all the same'.

Some of the stories of Corrymeela were heart-rending. One young boy, Tommy, saw his father shot dead by British troops. Tommy and his brothers were taken to Corrymeela, away from the grief of the home. Tommy had said nothing after his father had died. He was so shocked. But when he came to Corrymeela it was as if a tiny animal had emerged from a dark room into the sunlight.

Tommy went berserk. He was virtually uncontrollable until a friend of Corrymeela, a doctor, asked Tommy to guard a golf ball for him. He went to bed clutching that golf ball. Then the next night it was a golf ball and a golf club. Gradually he learnt how to relate again.

Later on, tragedy struck the same family when one of Tommy's brothers, was taken away and shot dead by terrorists. Another brother, who was with him shortly before he was killed, was brought to Corrymeela, and for days he was inconsolable.

Ray Davey, practically at his wit's end, asked him what could he do. 'Will you take me to see my brother's grave?', he asked. Ray agreed and they drove off to Belfast the next day. The boy spent a long time at the grave. He cried long and hard. When he came back to Corrymeela his grief began to subside. It was as if he could not believe his brother had died until he had seen the grave.

Yet there were other stories at Corrymeela which brought a smile to the lips. During one of the family weeks, a transistor radio and £25 were stolen shortly after one family arrived. The Corrymeela workers soon traced the culprit and the money and the radio were returned to their owners. The next morning everybody was wakened prematurely by the sight and the sound of a nearby hay field on fire. It was panic stations until the fire was extinguished. The culprit was the same small boy who had stolen the radio and the money on the previous day.

Ray Davey, in his towering majesty as Leader, delivered a stern lecture to the boy. 'How on earth did you manage to do it?', he asked, with weary rhetoric.

'I used matches', said the wee boy. 'But it took nine matches to get the damn thing started'.

On another occasion the patient and long-suffering members of Ballycastle Golf Club sent a deputation to Corrymeela to ask what had happened to their flags which disappeared off the greens during the night. Ray Davey was on the point of explaining that it couldn't possibly be his boys, when his eyes caught sight of a golf flag peeping out of a nearby whinbush...

Across the broad spectrum, Corrymeela has not dealt alone with the symptoms of violence or estrangement. It has been concerned with the causes and, if possible, the cures. The architects of a splintered society are as important as its victims. The Corrymeela Encounter projects have embraced a wide range of issues, social, political, cultural and theological. They have included 'The Generation Gap'; 'The Two Cultures'; 'The Arts in Ulster'; 'The Worker and the Church in a Changing Society'; 'Violence'; 'The Church Inside Out'; 'Ireland, a New Start'; 'Schools in Northern Ireland'; 'Police and Community'; 'Mixed Marriage'; 'One-Parent Families'; 'The Use of Television'; 'Ulster Politics and Christian Morality'. The number and the quality of the conferences have been due largely to the Rev. Harold Good, and his colleagues. They have tried, and in many cases succeeded, in showing the essential bridge between theory and practice. Some of the conferences have led to the formation of an organization to continue the discussion begun at Corrymeela. These include the Mixed Marriage Association,

the One-Parent Family Association and the Voluntary Housing Association. Again the conferences at Corrymeela are backed up by continuing study groups in Belfast, and once a month a Corrymeela Focus is held in Belfast to enable everyone who has been at Ballycastle to keep in touch.

Many people do keep in touch with Corrymeela. Each person who comes to Corrymeela brings something to the Community in his or her own way. Perhaps they derive something from it as well—perhaps an inspiration, certainly an insight into Corrymeela, which in turn helps to inspire those still working on the front line.

Father Frank Culhane, an Irishman who has visited Corrymeela, gave his own sharp reaction in a broadcast from Lausanne. Father Culhane, the priest in charge of the English-speaking Roman Catholic community there, said:

> More than a place, Corrymeela is a Community, a spirit, a movement of Christian men and women from all branches of the Church, who are committed to heal the many breaches, social, religious and political, which exist in Northern Ireland and throughout the world.

> It is one of those places where you find God in a privileged way because you are looking for Him in someone else quite different from yourself and your own tradition... I met on leaving the house, six young children coming up the road. Their father had been killed in the troubles a short time before. Their mother needed urgent hospital treatment, and it was Corrymeela that received these little victims of our politico-sectarian strife.

> Catholic orphans being cared for by young Protestant girls: a witness that our divisions are senseless and that if we are divided, Christ is not.

73

Stretching Out

On a blustery afternoon in October 1973, a light 'plane flew slowly across the sky in North Holland. Below were the small, tidy towns of Beverwijk, Castricum and Heemskerk, lying parallel to the canals and dikes thirty miles North of Amsterdam. As the red and white Cessna 'plane crossed the clear blue sky it dragged behind it a long red and white banner with a message in Dutch 'Help Noord Irse Kinde'—'Help Northern Ireland children'.

The flight was part of the fund-raising campaign organized by members of Dutch and Northern Irish Lions Clubs. The proceeds were for the work of the Corrymeela Community. Corrymeela had entered the European scene in style. A few years after its foundation, Corrymeela became known for its work in Church circles in Germany, Holland, Switzerland and the United States. Its reputation had reached centres as far apart as Norway and Peru, Hong Kong, Jordan and Canada, Russia, Australia, Sweden, India, Singapore and New Zealand. In some places abroad Corrymeela is now better known than in some parts of its native land.

Corrymeela's international links were tenuous at first but they became strengthened. The network has grown steadily. The word has spread in many ways. The international workcamps in conjunction with the World Council of Churches have been important sources of communication. Each camp has catered for about twenty young people, and many of these have brought back to their homelands the spirit of Corrymeela. Some of this information was picked up by the local press, and slowly the name of Corrymeela began to creep into the reports in papers and periodicals abroad.

Much was done by personal contact. Mark Gibbs of the Audenshaw Foundation, which publishes internationally papers on matters affecting the laity and the Church, became extremely interested. It was Gibbs who published the first international article about Corrymeela, in one of the Audenshaw Papers. Called 'For such a time as this', it was the fore-runner of a number of such papers giving an updated account of Corrymeela's progress in the midst of the Irish troubles.

One significant result of the contact established with Gibbs was an invitation to Ray Davey to take part in a one-day conference at St George's House, Windsor, with the leaders of British groups of lay centres. Davey accepted the invitation. At the start he had a 'brush' with the warden, a retired rear-admiral who met him at the entrance to the elegant building.

'So they let you out of Ireland, did they?' asked the rear-admiral whimsically.

'Yes', said Davey with the dourness of an Ulsterman who had been touched on a raw nerve. 'I have come to England to sort out a few of the problems here. This is where ours all began.' After that they became friends.

The most important contact at the conference was with Canon Horace Dammers of Coventry Cathedral; Dammers, now Dean of Bristol, has tremendous personal charm and attraction. Ray Davey spoke to the conference simply and briefly about Corrymeela. Dammers expressed an interest in the work and later when he was in Northern Ireland on business he took time off to visit Corrymeela. The visit had far-reaching consequences.

Shortly afterwards, the Provost of Canterbury invited Corrymeela to become a Cross of Nails Centre. It was an invitation, in effect, to join an international network of reconciliation with some fifty centres scattered all over the globe. Each, in association with the Cross of Nails, serves a common vision and a ministry of hope.

The Cross of Nails idea originated amid the ruins of the ancient Coventry Cathedral which was destroyed by German bombers during World War II. A member of the Cathedral staff was sifting through the charred ruins when he found three of the massively long nails of mediaeval design. He placed the nails end to end, with their heads touching, and he put the third nail across the other two. Thus the Cross of Nails was born, and it became a symbol of reconciliation. After the War, Germany was chosen as the first contact and a deep and lasting relationship was established between

Coventry and Dresden, both of which had suffered so terribly during the War. The people of Dresden raised money and built an international centre at Coventry Cathedral. The Cathedral responded by raising money and it sent volunteers to rebuild their hospital which had been devastated by bombs. The Cross of Nails was becoming a world-wide symbol and from it a global network was being established.

In September 1971 Canon Horace Dammers himself came over to Corrymeela to present a replica of the Cross of Nails. It was a simple ceremony on a bright Saturday afternoon. With gusts of wind whirling about the headland at Ballycastle, five hundred people gathered at Corrymeela. They included believers from the main Protestant Churches and the Roman Catholic Church. The Corrymeela Community did not want it to be a domestic occasion for its own members, but rather a call to the whole community. The letter of invitation read: 'We ask all Christian people to join the prayers with ours for peace and justice in our land'. Members of Parliament, both from Westminster and Stormont, were invited. Significantly, only one of them came. Two others sent apologies.

The Cross of Nails service had little ceremony and no music. Four members of the Community read the words of Christ, the local Catholic priest led prayers for forgiveness, a Presbyterian minister said prayers for peace. The Cross of Nails was carried in the midst of the people. Ray Davey read the words of Christ: 'You shall love the Lord your God with all your heart, and with all your soul, and with all your mind. This is the great and first commandment'. Then everyone shook hands with their neighbours to symbolize the act of reconciliation, and the ceremony was over.

To the members of Corrymeela the gift was more than a friendly gesture from Coventry. It was a recall to the Community's basis and inspiration. It was a challenge; was Corrymeela doing enough? Was it adventurous enough? Was it thinking big, or small?

There was no doubt that Coventry Cathedral was thinking big. It made the work of Corrymeela one of its main appeals and its members undertook to raise money for a Coventry House of Reconciliation. This was to be a large centre for residential groups, both long and short term, and it was and is regarded as one of Corrymeela's most urgent needs and greatest assets. Members of Coventry Cathedral set about raising money with great determination. Canon Horace Dammers and the Rev. Ken Woolhouse, the Cathedral's Education Officer, wrote to individual firms, to churches, to groups all over the world and to financial trusts. They raised £30,000, and the Coventry House of Reconciliation is a tangible symbol of caring. That caring had been witnessed in places many thousands of miles away. Horace Dammers received a letter from a Benedictine Monastery in Lima, Peru, which underlined the priorities of life and death in no uncertain fashion. The letter read: 'Thank you very much for the leaflet concerning your work for Christian reconciliation in Northern Ireland. We are praying for your work there.

'At the present time our priory is undergoing reconstruction. Two-and-a-half years ago it was completely destroyed. That was not bad. What hurt were the 75,000 people who died in our earthquake. Our losses were slight in comparison, four of the sisters and seven of our students and the Superior. For one year we have lived in tents at 10,500 feet above sea level, and six months of the year we had heavy rains. Only last year we were able to get the Sisters' Convent rebuilt, reconstruct a monastery, and find financial support to finish a part of our school. Rebuilding has taken all the money we had, to do these small works. We feel very much as St Peter—silver, gold, there is none that I have but in Christ Jesus, a blessing upon you and your good works'.

In 1973 Coventry Cathedral organized two special international workcamps at Corrymeela to prepare the ground physically for the House of Reconciliation. Some of the toil, the sweat and the satisfaction of the work has been described in the international magazine 'Network'.

Rose Marie Depp, an American girl, wrote: 'I think Corrymeela's success, if one can be presumptuous and call it that, is due to the belief on the part of its leaders in the need for a person's own reconciliation in life before he can hope to bring it to society and between men. The staff and workers have to share their experience and not preach an ideal'.

Sue Parker, a member of Coventry Cathedral, wrote: 'We had encountered a great deal of fear (in Northern Ireland), but also a tremendous hope. Corrymeela is part of that hope. Its effect on me was so great that I shall be going back. Coventry means a lot to Corrymeela—both now mean a lot to me'.

In this, and in many other ways, the reputation of Corrymeela began to spread. The Leader, Ray Davey, was asked to speak at meetings in Scotland and England, then to a series of conferences in London. Then came an invitation to Germany and several meetings were held in the Wuppertal-Barmen area. This was a centre for the Confessional Church which had stood out so courageously against Nazism. In 1934 a number of church leaders and pastors signed the Barmen Declaration. It stated that the loyalty which Nazism demanded was incompatible with loyalty to Christ.

Many of the people who signed that Declaration were later to die in concentration camps. Frau Vikarin Haerter, a pastor of the Confessional Church, had heard about Corrymeela and she invited Ray Davey to Germany. Davey found his audience sympathetic and understanding, but it was he who was impressed by them. He said later: 'Bearing in mind their background and their history, I felt that I had more to learn from them than they from me.'

The German visit culminated in a flight from Hannover to Berlin where Davey met Dr. Franz von Hammerstein, the leader of 'Aktion Suehnezeichen', (literally 'Action Reconciliation'). The nearest equivalent in Britain is Voluntary Service Overseas, or in America the Kennedy Peace Corps. In the German organization, young people who do not wish to take part in military service are allowed to work at projects outside Germany that foster reconciliation. As a result of Davey's meeting with von Hammerstein, a steady stream of Germans came to Corrymeela. Each in his or her own way made some contribution and they may have found something in Corrymeela to bring back with them. Often the real contribution to international visitors has been to maintain contact with Corrymeela and its work long after they had left Ballycastle or Belfast. For example, Maurice Meillard, a Swiss student, returned to Lausanne and became a local ambassador for Corrymeela. It was through Meillard that Ray Davey was invited to Lausanne for the Week of Prayer for Christian Unity. He was accompanied by Father Tony Farquhar, one of the Catholic Chaplains at Queen's University. In eight days they spoke to more than twenty-four groups of people.

They met the press many times and spoke to television and radio journalists who were keen to know what Corrymeela was doing and, more important, its chances of influencing a permanent settlement. Davey and Farquhar spoke in churches, church halls, in a superb modern theatre, and, on one occasion, in Lausanne Cathedral.

They found their audiences deeply attentive. There was a genuine desire to try to understand. Links were formed and later strengthened. In Geneva the Irishmen met Dr. Philip Potter, the General Secretary of the World Council of Churches. He showed a real interest in the Northern Ireland situation and later visited Corrymeela. At Lausanne they met Father Frank Culhane. One important result of that visit was a donation to help support financially one worker at Corrymeela each year. This money is still being raised and the effort of Frank Culhane's small community in Switzerland is deeply appreciated by Corrymeela in Ireland.

The fact that a Roman Catholic priest and a Presbyterian minister could share the same platform or pulpit impressed many in Europe who had believed that Catholics and Protestants in Northern Ireland had no real contact with one another. It would be an oversimplification to suggest that one Presbyterian minister and one priest on the same platform minimized the extraordinarily complex problem of people in Northern Ireland, but to foreign eyes it symbolized that reconciliation in Ireland was already taking place in specific, though limited, areas.

At times the two Irishmen were like innocents abroad. At the Ecumenical Club in Geneva they were sitting beside a very pretty Oriental girl. She looked extremely young, and one of the Irishmen asked her which school she attended. She replied, without batting an eyelid, that she was the Vietnamese Ambassador. 'Oh?', said the Irishman, 'fancy that now'.

On another occasion Farquhar and Davey were shown round the very beautiful Romanesque church in Romainmôtier. In the vestry they noticed a large map showing the movement of missionaries from Ireland right across Europe. It was shattering for Davey and Farquhar to realize that both of them, each of his own tradition, had come centuries later to Switzerland to try to explain to Christians in Europe what had gone wrong in Ireland.

The trips to Switzerland and Germany had been mainly for information, but the visit to Holland was financially rewarding. The Lions Clubs in Holland had worked hard to raise money. By the time Davey flew into Holland for the final stage of the campaign, there were reminders of Northern Ireland everywhere. Every shop in the three towns displayed posters, there were posters on every bus, there was a large visual display with enlarged photographs of Corrymeela. There were door-to-door collections, fund-raising speeches and personal appearances reminiscent more of show-business than the Irish troubles.

The response from the Dutch people was generous, and the money helped the Corrymeela Community to establish a recreation centre at Ballycastle. Ray Davey thanked his hosts and said that people in Ireland were amazed that others in Europe should care to that extent. Davey was told that the Dutch, with their own history of polarization, felt they knew something about the realities of reconciliation and they were anxious to help.

Between the European visits, Davey and Farquhar went to America, again on an information basis. People there were anxious to hear something about the other side of Northern Ireland. Most media news, by its nature, is bad news and the tiny snippets of good news that did come from Ireland were in danger of being crowded out of the bulletins. In twenty-eight days, Davey and Farquhar, with the help of an Irish student folk group called Scorpio, covered 10,000 miles. They presented their Irish scenario on radio and television, they gave numerous press interviews. They spoke to audiences in hospitals, universities and seminaries, in colleges, churches and chapels, Ecumenical centres and Rotary Clubs. Their audiences included some IRA sympathizers and some hard-line Unionist supporters. The visit was exhausting, but Farquhar and Davey felt it had been worthwhile to present another picture to a wider audience, and they in turn learnt much from their American experiences.

The development of Corrymeela within the British context has also been very important. Already it had built-in contacts through Iona and Coventry. But a most important development has been the establishment of the London Corrymeela Venture. This began through the initiative of two neighbouring parishes in London—Christ Church, Lancaster Gate (Church of England) and Holy Rosary on the Old Marylebone Road (Roman Catholic). They wanted to do something to help in Northern Ireland and they brought mixed groups of Belfast children to London for holidays. The London workers felt, however, that this activity had limited effects. Holidays for children were fine, but once the children returned to Belfast the stresses of the old environment appeared once again.

So the London group decided to do something different and if possible something that would be more permanent. Several members came to Northern Ireland in 1973 and they visited Corrymeela. After careful consideration, the decision was taken to support the Community from London, and the London Corrymeela Venture was born.

A most active committee was formed and the determination of the new venture was shown in the plan to stage a year-long appeal. A full-time secretary, Mrs. Pam Reeves, was appointed, office premises were rented and the campaign was officially launched by Mr. William Whitelaw, the former Secretary of State for Northern Ireland who himself had almost achieved the impossible by persuading many of the politicians there to reconcile their differences. Those obstacles, as has been seen, proved insurmountable.

The London Corrymeela Venture set itself high targets, and its range of fund-raising activities has been an inspiration and indeed a challenge to the Corrymeela

Centre back in Ireland. It includes house-to-house collections, the establishment of collection rotas at Paddington Station, London exhibitions of Corrymeela works, vigils, concerts, premieres, and other fund-raising activities. In a most practical way the seed of the Ballycastle and Belfast Corrymeela has taken root near the heart of one of the world's great cities.

Corrymeela has also developed links with the Irish Republic, a development that is singularly appropriate to an Irish-based community dedicated to crossing all the borders. A Corrymeela group of about thirty people was formed from staff and students at Trinity College Dublin. The members travel regularly to Belfast and Ballycastle. In turn the Northern Ireland staff visit Dublin for briefing sessions.

The Dublin Corrymeela Group is much smaller than its Northern counterpart. What it lacks in numbers it maintains in influence as one of the several reconciliation and peace groups which are working together in the Irish Republic. They have been playing a key role in promoting peace rallies and they have been working in those areas of Irish life where the social need is greatest. One of the tangible results of their work has been the establishment of the Glencree Centre outside Dublin which, like Corrymeela, is dedicated to reconciliation. Ray Davey was one of the main speakers at the opening ceremony in 1974. He said: 'My only qualification for speaking to you today is that I have been part of the Corrymeela Community which has been for some years doing similar work. Our own Dublin group is involved with you in this work and I am glad to bring the good wishes of the members of our Community in the North...

'This country of ours, both North and South, cherishes many symbols. But all too often they speak of the past and they tend to keep us looking back instead of forward. I think today of a prayer by a great Scottish theologian—"let not the past ever be so dear to us as to set a limit to the future." It is a prayer for all Irishmen today.'

That prayer is being echoed by all kinds of Irishmen, and one link which Corrymeela values particularly in the Irish Republic is that with the Irish School of Ecumenics in Dublin. Several of the members have contributed to the work of Corrymeela, personally, practically, intellectually and inspirationally. Corrymeela has been the richer because of their involvement.

Internationally, Corrymeela would appear to have progressed remarkably since its establishment in 1965. It is known in Christian circles in many parts of the world, it receives money from various places, it is regarded internationally by those who know it as an exponent of universal caring Christianity. But what is its true significance internationally?

Its international reputation has brought it only limited finance. Judged as a fund-raising exercise, the visits abroad have been comparative failures, apart from the Dutch venture which was specifically to raise money. The American trip raised barely more than enough to pay for the expenses. Any organization dedicated to making money could hardly have failed to have done better.

Money continues to come in from many sources. One day it could be from a congregation in Ohio, on another day from friends in Germany or Switzerland or

Holland or Great Britain. Even the Queen of England instructed the Keeper of the Privy Purse to send a donation. It was small, but it was a donation from the Queen of England. Many of the financial gifts are small, apart from the exceptional help from Coventry Cathedral and Dutch friends.

But Corrymeela is not about money alone. And, to be fair, those who carried the message of Corrymeela to Europe were invited abroad on a purely information basis. They had not set out to raise vast sums. The Corrymeela philosophy sounds naive to a hard-headed businessman, but it is very much Corrymeela—'We feel that we will get the financial support required so long as our cause is felt to be right'.

The international significance of Corrymeela is a two-way process. It hopes to remind Christians and non-Christians outside Ireland that there is another side to the Irish story. And in turn, Christians and non-Christians outside Ireland give the members of the Corrymeela Community an outward dimension that enables them to look outside their own local problems.

Corrymeela itself was conceived and established on an international basis. Some of its members visited Agape, Riesi and Taizé, others brought to Corrymeela their own experience of other parts of the world. And visiting students from abroad also made valuable contributions, though it must be said that some have not. There is always the danger that Corrymeela attracts the ecumenically curious and trendy. Some people have looked on Corrymeela as a one-way ticket to an Irish holiday where talk was more important than words. Others were too lazy to get off their backsides and do the repetitive drudgery that is so much part of the continuous servicing of Corrymeela. Yet others were hardly mature enough to be able to add much to a demanding political, social and human situation. The old maxim still applies: 'There is no point in sending under-developed people to under-developed countries'. Fortunately the Corrymeela misfits have been in the minority. The core of Corrymeela's international involvement has been the inspiration it has given to members of the Community in Ireland. The visits by Ray Davey and others to Europe and America were physically exhausting but intellectually challenging. They met the people who asked the questions. In America they encountered IRA sympathizers who were not convinced that reconciliation is the answer in Ireland. They met hard-line Unionists who felt that the answer to the IRA was ruthless military repression and that Corrymeela was only meddling by putting forward its ideas of reconciliation. In Germany they met people who believed that the Irish problem could be explained in Marxist terms. In all these countries they met people, particularly lay people, who asked them when on earth Irish people were going to come to their senses.

It was not enough to tell all these different types of people that Corrymeela was a community of nice folk trying to do good works. Corrymeela is much more than that, and Davey and his helpers were continually forced to develop their philosophies in the light of new information and new challenges. Above all, the international involvement has helped to reassure the Corrymeela Community that people do care, in the words of the Apostle Paul: 'If one member suffers, all suffer together. If one member is honoured, all rejoice together'.

Dr. Garret FitzGerald, the voluble and much-travelled Irish Foreign Minister would not claim to have the endurance of St. Paul, even though he may be held in equally high esteem in certain Dublin circles. FitzGerald in spite of his folksy approach is a shrewd commentator on Northern Irish affairs and in a newspaper article he sketched neatly the outsider's and the cross-border view of Corrymeela at work. He said:

> From outside, the Northern scene appears a dark one, capable of undermining faith in humanity. But to one brought into touch, casually or by design, with the healing and constructive work of so very many totally committed people, the message of Northern Ireland is very different. To leave the North after such a visit to Corrymeela is not something one does with relief at returning to normality and to relative safety: instead one crosses into the Republic with regret, a sense of loss, and an urgent desire to return as soon as possible and share even vicariously in what is happening across the Border...

> There is a contrast too between the horror of a conflict based on religion as a dividing factor, which never ceases to turn one's stomach, and the living sense of Christian witness amongst so many of those involved in constructive work. Prayer has a new meaning in this context—above all, it must be said, inter-denominational prayer. One senses that in face of the all-pervading bigotry, many of those who are giving themselves in a spirit of love to their shattered society find their strength in praying together with their colleagues of other Christian denominations. To pray thus in the present atmosphere of Northern Ireland can be an unbearably moving experience, equally for those visiting the province as for those living and working there.

> ...the only unity worth having in this island will be a unity based on this universal love. If we cannot now make the effort to join at least in spirit with those who, in the difficult climate of the North, are practising universal love, Ireland will not merely remain divided: it will be torn asunder.

In a real sense Corrymeela has been beyond Ireland and if it had not been able to stretch out internationally it would have died. The love of God is universal and Corrymeela would have no right to claim, nor would it want to claim, that love and reconciliation is for Irishmen alone. Ray Davey was not thinking about Ireland or Irishmen only when he remarked after one of his visits abroad: 'The penny has to drop some time that reconciliation is what Christianity is all about. If we Christians cannot speak the message of reconciliation, who can? Otherwise we have nothing to say.'

God's Question-mark

When Tullio Vinay spoke at the opening of Corrymeela in 1965, he said that he hoped it would be 'a question-mark to the Church everywhere'. Corrymeela has tried to fulfill this role. Its programme of activities indicates what it believes Christian reconciliation should be about. Corrymeela has been supported by some church leaders, by some churches and by some church members. But in trying to be a practical example of 'God's question-mark', Corrymeela continues to lay itself open to misunderstanding.

What Corrymeela has tried to say has been said by those who have not written off the churches. It is said in the hope that the various churches will throw off their captivity to political ideologies and will speak seminal and radical words of forgiveness, peace and love. These words are proclaimed by every denomination in Ireland. Properly understood and acted upon they can bring the sort of communal healing and trust upon which a permanent peace in Ireland could be built. Corrymeela is seeing more clearly the cost of such a witness.

The role of Corrymeela has been likened to that of paratroopers to the main forces of an army. If that analogy is valid, it means that Corrymeela must live a life of tension. There is tension, on the one hand between its role of pushing out, probing new frontiers, breaking new ground; and on the other hand, of keeping in contact with the main body of troops who are often more cautious and slower to move. This is a vital role for Corrymeela. To perform it properly, freedom is essential; freedom for all sorts of experiment and research, freedom to take risks in new types of programmes, and freedom to hold discussions with all sorts of groups with widely differing outlooks.

Corrymeela also needs to keep in touch with the churches, listening to what they have to say and interpreting what others want to say. Corrymeela is in a frontier position, interpreting the Church to people outside, and trying to make the churches and church people aware of and sensitive to the attitudes and ideas of those outside.

Corrymeela is partly a protest group within the churches. It is a protest against the inflexibility, the institutionalism, the authoritarianism and the pietism of the churches. In this, Corrymeela is expressing what an ever-increasing number of young people are thinking today. A report on sixth-form religion in Northern Ireland by the Rev. Dr. John Greer, the Church of Ireland chaplain and a lecturer in religious education at the New University of Ulster, was startling because of the clarity of the criticism expressed by young people. 'The ideal in politics is not that the Church should guide and control the politics of any country, but that those in charge of Government (no matter whether Protestant or Catholic), should be Christians, practising Christian lives'. Or again, 'The Church in Northern Ireland has far too much influence on politics, resulting in a situation where members of one church are naturally assumed to vote for a particular party'. And again, 'all churches are primarily concerned with the maintenance of their own machines and have lost their mission as a servant of the community'. Or again, 'the Church in Ireland caters for a section of the community who don't think for themselves'. And finally, 'Teach us about life. Religion should be questioned, not asserted. If it is true it will become stronger for being questioned, if not it will be destroyed'.

Corrymeela in its conferences and its programmes poses these kinds of questions. Will the institutional churches in Ireland look at themselves courageously and openly, examining their structures and their calling as the servants of Christ to the whole community? Are the present structures helping to heal the divisions in this country and to break down the barriers of misunderstanding and mistrust, or do they merely serve to maintain and fortify the divisions? There are many people who argue that the latter applies.

The Rev. John Morrow, the Presbyterian Chaplain of Trinity College, Dublin, and a Corrymeela foundermember, puts his criticism pungently in an Audenshaw Paper 'The Captivity of the Irish Churches'. He writes: 'The history of Ireland has conspired to support a near identity of our political and religious communities. The Reformation struggle, the seventeenth century plantation of settlers in Ulster, and the identification of the Roman Catholic Church with the plight of the dispossessed of that period have all proved to be of enduring significance. The struggle for political independence from Britain has tended to cement those relationships and to maintain the sharpness of our basic divisions. Father Patrick Daigan in 'The Irish Conflict and the Christian Conscience' summed up the situation by saying that 'the people of Northern Ireland are the most conspicuous victims of several historic ruptures in human relations, not all peculiar to Ulster or to Ireland, but all reinforcing one another there as nowhere else'. There have been periods and episodes in Irish Church history where a spirit of self criticism was fairly marked, for example among Presbyterians in the eighteenth century, but it must be conceded that, however complex the reasons, the majority of church leaders and members have become captive to the political ideologies of Unionism or Nationalism to such a degree that they are unable to make a clear distinction between commitment to their faith and commitment to a particular political viewpoint.

'We appear to have sold our spiritual independence for the support of our members, and have been impotent to challenge the latent sectarianism and tribalism in Northern Ireland with the transcendent viewpoint of the Gospel'.

At the extremes, this inter-relation between religion and party politics is neatly illustrated by slogans from each side of the divide. Hard-line Protestants from the Vanguard Unionist Progressive Party claim that their party is 'For God, for Queen, for Ulster'. Republicans include in death notices for departed comrades 'Mary, Mother of Ireland, pray for him'. In each case divine approval is assumed to accompany territorial and political aspirations.

This interaction of religion and politics is shown less starkly but no less significantly in the actions of some leading churchmen. Those who criticize the Orange Order for its close identification with Unionist party politics will not fail to note that the Grand Master of the Grand Orange Lodge of Ireland is a Presbyterian Minister. And when the Moderator of the General Assembly attends the opening ceremony at an Orange Order headquarters many people inside and outside the Presbyterian Church question the attitude of that entire church in general to the Protestant supremacy implied by the Orange Order. The Moderator may claim that he attended the function in a private capacity, but as the Moderator of the Presbyterian Assembly he has a public responsibility to all sections of the Church that over-rides his privileges as a private citizen. (There are many Presbyterians, however, who would feel that a Moderator had a perfectly proper place on an Orange platform.)

Insensitivity to the interaction of religion and politics is not confined to one side alone. Many Protestants would find it difficult to understand why the Most Rev. Dr. Dermot Ryan, the Roman Catholic Archbishop of Dublin, and his predecessor the Most Rev. Dr. John McQuaid, went to the bedside of Sean McStiofain, a provisional IRA leader, who was fasting to death in a Dublin hospital. The Archbishops may have felt that a request from an intermediary to visit a 'dying' man was one that no Christian could ignore, but to Protestant eyes their visit confirmed what many non-Catholics in the North have seen as a tacit Roman Catholic approval for the Provisional IRA. The Rt. Rev. Dr. Edward Daly, the young and forward-looking Roman Catholic Bishop of Derry, said repeatedly that he was against excommunicating the IRA on the grounds that once the Church cut off contact with people it ceased to have any influence on them. Such an argument is not irrational, but to many Protestants it would be further evidence of the Roman Catholic hierarchy's alleged lack of conviction in speaking out against the IRA.

Professor J. C. Beckett, in a paper presented to the Church of Ireland Synod in Dublin in 1975, claimed that the Roman Catholic Church, 'for all practical purposes ... is politically committed; it is identified with the policy of bringing the Six-County area under the control of a Government in Dublin. This is the declared policy of the Roman Catholic political party in the North as well as all parties in the South. In other words, Roman Catholics on both sides of the border represent, on this critical issue, a single point of view'. On the other side, the Rev. Ashley Smith, a Jamaican, wrote of his visit to Northern Ireland in 1973:

> Most Protestants with whom I have spoken lead me to believe that they know what is basically wrong with Northern Ireland but maintain an attitude to the situation which seems to be a mixture of guilt, self-deception and insecurity. From all appearances, the average Presbyterian knows that there is something untenable about the traditional 'Unionist' position in Northern Ireland but refuses to accept the necessity for a change in the *status quo* because he is so concerned about his status in a new situation that is qualitatively different from the present. It is true that these fears are common to all groups but their debilitating effect must not be overlooked.

> After observing the proceedings of the 1973 General Assembly of the Presbyterian Church, one is tempted to think that the militancy in much of the evangelicalism might be directed not so much at bringing of Salvation to those who are outsiders to the Faith as to maintaining the present political and economic position of non-Catholics in Northern Ireland, despite the obvious

97

evil effects that this has upon the entire community. The expressed zeal for the defence of the 'Word of God' is not seen to be matched by the charitableness and meekness of Him on whose Life, Suffering, Death and Resurrection the evangelical faith is based. One gets the impression that there is a tendency for the Word of God to be 'pressed into service' in support of the ideological position of a particular group.

One is, therefore, at one and the same time delighted at the charming Christ-likeness of so many who are prepared to bear the cross for Christ's sake, and depressed by what might be described as the open defiance of Christ by some, in the determination to maintain 'enemy' relationships with fellow citizens.

Such painfully honest comments from an outside observer fortify the arguments that the institutional churches in Ireland, despite the work of individuals in those churches, have intensified the divisions in Irish society.

Some people—and particularly churchmen—have claimed that the Ulster conflict is not about religion, but about social and political problems. There is some truth in this. But it is misleading to claim that religion is not a basic contributory factor. Dr. Conor Cruise O'Brien, one of the more informed Dublin politicians on Northern affairs, has noted 'if religion is a red herring, then it is a herring about as big as a whale'.

The point is made in another way in 'Tribalism or Christianity in Ireland?'. It states:

To claim, as did recent statements by the four church leaders, that violence in Ireland has no religious roots but can be attributed to social, economic, political and historical forces is unacceptable... The justification for the statement would seem to be to preserve us from too critical a scrutiny by world christendom which increasingly is uneasy about the reality of the 'Protestant-Catholic religious element' in our troubles. Irish Christianity is an embarassment to non-Irish Christians; we are a stumbling block to missionary endeavour elsewhere in the world.

Tribal religion in Ireland has been so endemic that the members of both tribes have often failed to recognize it because they never sought nor experienced anything better. Ireland has been plagued by religion. Ireland has served Christianity badly.

Tony Spencer, a Queen's University sociologist, in his controversial article for 'The Month' of June 1973, gave his interpretation of the political-religious link in practice.

> The political institutions of the Catholic community see to it that nothing is done to weaken the immense power of the Catholic Church over its own members. This is seen in the unique degree of clerical control over the education system of the Republic and over the Catholic system in the North. It is seen in the rigorous interpretation and application of the mixed-marriage rules, and in the Church's strict control over family life and procreation...

> ...In return for political subservience and acquiescence in Church power, the political institutions of the Catholic community get a great deal. Catholicism is the key to the Irish national identity, as the clergy are never tired of insisting.

> ...This implicit alliance is not, however, completely unlimited. There is a critical cut-off point. Historically, this has been reached when a rising level of politically-motivated violence in the Irish Catholic community evokes fears in Rome about the most sacred values of Christianity. The bishops then begin issuing denunciations of violence, highly qualified at first but more explicit as the violence increases. The denunciations are seen as rituals imposed on bishops whose difficulties must be understood'. They have little effect on those engaged in or supporting violence. When it is all over, episcopal disloyalty is quickly forgiven and the Catholic community becomes once more extremely sensitive to episcopal opinion on every conceivable topic.

> In the Protestant Scots-Irish community of the North the alliance works differently. The Protestant churches are extremely weak. Exposed to the power of the Catholic Church they could expect to crumble quickly if they were not protected by the political institutions. So Unionism has provided a school system that inculcates an Ulster Protestant identity as effectively as the Catholic Church-controlled system produces an Irish Catholic identity...

It controls immigration, so that Catholics from the Republic are kept out. By a very effective system of discrimination in housing and employment it protected Protestants from the displacement and enforced emigration occasioned by the very high Catholic fertility. And by dint of gerrymandering and plural voting, the power was kept in Protestant hands.

There does not seem to be a clear cut-off point in the Protestant community, probably because the greater autonomy of the Protestant churches makes them less responsive to external concern for the sacred core values of Christianity. Geneva and Canterbury do not have to be placated as Rome does. In what is seen as a struggle for survival, the cut-off point tends to be more of an individual one. A Protestant minister reaches it when he can no longer endure what he has come to recognize as the desecration of Christianity. He makes his protest; his congregation makes life impossible for him; he quits.

Whatever churchmen may say in defence of their own institution, the hard fact remains that the tragedy of the Irish churches is their failure over the years to promulgate a Christianity that can cross all the barriers. Irishmen and women in every small town and village know who 'the other side' are. Everyone knows the minority partner in a mixed marriage. Everyone, or nearly everyone, is aware of, or wants to be aware of, the other man's religion, because that religion is the short-hand note to the other person's education, background and often his political views.

There are exceptions, but generally among the main body of church attenders in both traditions there is ignorance, fear and suspicion of the other. Certain efforts at closer co-operation have been frowned upon. Many excuses are offered, many efforts are made to put the blame elsewhere. But the bald fact remains that the churches collectively have failed to bring about the kind of reconciliation and acceptance that could enable the community to live pluralistically and peacefully. In April 1975 a joint consultation of the British and Irish Churches, meeting at Newcastle, Co. Down, suggested, among other things, the provision of or the support by the churches as such of a centre of reconciliation in Ireland. The proposal was well meant but the very fact that it was made underlined how little the major churches have done collectively in the past. Dean Swift's bitter jibe of so long ago still applies today: 'We have just enough to religion to make us hate, and not enough to make us love one another.'

The separate development between the two main Christian traditions has had a deep influence on both. It has helped to keep them both conservative, and resistant to change. There is the solid opposition of many Protestants to anything ecumenical. There is the lack of enthusiasm among many Catholics for much of Vatican II. The religious stalemate provides one of the reasons why so many denominations stress the importance of personal belief and salvation, but stop there. Both sin and salvation are seen in personal terms. Corporate and social sin is underplayed as is the corporate idea of salvation. The 'saved' person has his puritanical ethic, with its emphasis on keeping the 'Sabbath', and the dangers of drink, gambling and sex. But his responsibilities in the wider world of industry, commerce and politics are either ignored or misunderstood. Such a limited idea of salvation can leave the subject self-centred and vulnerable to exploitation by extremist politicians, who can use religious language as a cloak for un-Christian attitudes and actions.

Socially there is also the danger that the churches are speaking mainly to the middle classes but they have less influence among the men of violence from the inner-urban areas and the relatively new housing estates. In the Audenshaw Papers No. 36, an anonymous writer calling himself 'A Layman in dark Belfast', notes:

> Very many church people still restrict their activities very much to their local churches, by attending Sunday services, the prayer meetings, and the church organizations. This is virtually all they do. I am afraid that most of the people who are involved in local community organizations—especially in Belfast—have very few church contacts. And this is true also of middle-class Roman Catholics. If you are making a good salary, whether you are Protestant or Catholic, the conditions in the riot areas hardly seem to matter.

> ...By and large, the working class on both sides have simply a nominal affiliation with their churches. They have got a historical label, that is all. They pay very little attention to what their priests and ministers say, unless it is something they agree with anyway. I fear that this is just as true of the extreme Protestants as of the IRA 'Provisionals'; the churches seem to have lost touch both institutionally and on a personal level with many of the 'UDA types'.

There is a danger in generalizing in class terms but those who know the middle class and the working class Ulster may see more than a grain of truth in what the writer says. His argument is substantiated at another level. Despite repeated exhortations from church leaders, the men of violence continue to bomb, to shoot and to disrupt. It is impossible not to conclude the clerical seeds of wisdom have fallen on stony ground.

It is equally dangerous to write off every section of every church. Much work has been done at grass-roots level by individuals and by some church organizations. And a major personal initiative by four Protestant clergymen at Feakle, in County Clare, paved the way for a Provisional IRA ceasefire. (This initiative was backed later by the institutional churches that the men represented, but not without heartburnings by individuals. For example, the Moderator of the Presbyterian Church issued a personal statement pointing out that insofar as the Moderator may be regarded as a church leader, he was in no way involved in the Feakle talks.)

Again it would be wrong to overlook the tentative beginnings of dialogue between the Protestant and Catholic Churches as at the Interchurch meetings at Ballymascanlon, Dundalk. But at the meeting during the Spring of 1975 Mr. Barry Deane, a Church of Ireland member from Cork, asked was it a case of 'soft words at Ballymascanlon and a hard line at the grass-roots'.

Against such a background of church institutionalism and politico-religious involvement in Ireland, Corrymeela has moved cautiously. If the members of the Corrymeela Community were to be God's question-mark, or more graphically, God's paratroopers, there was no advantage in cutting off the supply lines to the church people at base. The point that Corrymeela made early on was that while it had neither a Catholic nor a non-Catholic theology, it did have a theology. Its statement of belief has been simple. 'We believe in God as revealed in Jesus Christ and in the continuing work of the Holy Spirit. We are called together as a Community to be an instrument of God's peace, to serve our society and to share in the life of the Church.' The Corrymeela joint worship is simple, and its simplicity has moved all sorts of people. It moved James Kelly, a senior journalist with a Dublin newspaper, to say in the presence of hard-bitten journalists at a conference on 'Media and the Community Conflict' that the Corrymeela people would be known by later generations as 'the saints of our time'. The spirit of Corrymeela also moved a Belfast teenager Ann McPartland, to translate potentially complex theology into a simple reality when she wrote 'Corrymeela is very important to me. It brings Christ right down on my level. I see Him in the people I meet in the community and so have grown to love Him'. Most important of all, Corrymeela has attempted to live its theology not just to discuss it. Ray Davey, the Corrymeela Leader, told his mixed audience of Catholics and Protestants and non-Christians at the opening of the Glencree Centre near Dublin in 1974: 'Talk and dialogue are alright provided they lead to something more. One of the factors that has made Corrymeela credible is not what we have said, but what we have tried to do; our programme for the families who perpetually live in fear and danger, the work of our young people for teenagers from the areas of violence, the support and the help we have tried to give to the relatives of the internees and intimidated on both sides'.

Corrymeela has tried to show what can be done in a simple, caring, Christian and non-denominational way. The essence of its conciliatory message was contained in a sermon at St. Patrick's Cathedral in Dublin by the Rev. Gabriel Daly, of the Irish School of Ecumenics. He said: 'The urge to reconcile and to be reconciled rises out of the conviction that we cannot be right with God while divisiveness is allowed to fester in our hearts. Only if we are taking reconciliation seriously in our family and neighbourhood, at work and among our acquaintances, are we likely to take it seriously in the wider political and national context.

Every effort to bring people together—anywhere and even in seemingly trivial ways—every effort of this kind is an attempt to advance the kingdom of God'.

Corrymeela has never identified itself with any political party. It is not because it believes politics are unimportant. Indeed many members are active in their own parties, but rather because it sees its role as that of trying to bring individuals and groups with different political and social attitudes together so that they may meet on a personal basis, get to know each other and to find areas of common concern and interest and see where their differences really lie.

So often the trouble can be that of ignorance, misunderstanding and lack of communication. In all this the Corrymeela Community, as a Christian centre, sees its role as partly that of providing a common ground. It attempts in a regular worship and the Community presence to witness that the different traditions can work together and that the fundamental message of the Gospel is that of forgiveness and reconciliation, a power that draws people together and breaks down the barriers rather than reinforcing tribalism and separation.

In trying to be God's question-mark, Corrymeela has asked some of the wrong questions. But it has asked many of the right questions. And the answers are still being worked out.

Beginning or End

It has been said that Corrymeela is an attitude of mind and a way of life. Yet the world will judge Corrymeela on the world's terms, on words like 'success' and 'achievement'. If some people are regarded as too earthly to be of any heavenly use the corollary is to be too heavenly for any earthly use. Perhaps the true Corrymeela fits somewhere in between.

Looked at critically, is the Corrymeela venture just a nice idea, promoted by nice people who have gained prominence because of the situation in Ireland? Does it lack depth and insight, so that it will fade like so many other movements that have been merely superficial? Or does Corrymeela represent something of permanent worth that transcends its age and its geographical base?

In practical terms there have been achievements. One point to note, though apparently obvious but sometimes understressed, is that Corrymeela has become a reality. It does exist. Corrymeela has happened. It keeps on growing. There is an increasing number of people, both Catholic and Protestant, who have learned to trust and to respect one another, who are glad to accept one another as fellow workers in a common love and concern for their country and its peoples. There are many who look on Corrymeela as a symbol of what can be done and as a sign of a new society that needs to be fashioned.

Corrymeela has attracted many young people, again no minor achievement in this modern age with its enormous pressures on the young. Most of the young people became interested in Corrymeela by taking part in the workcamps, and the Corrymeela message has been not only heard but experienced. In that sense the young people could identify with a man like Bonhoeffer, that Christian martyr in Nazi Germany, who said: 'To be a Christian is to be a disciple, not just an admirer or a talker'. Again the membership of Corrymeela is mostly of lay people. This is significant in an age when so many established structures, not least the churches, are being questioned. The future of the churches lies more and more in the rediscovery of the laity. In the words of Paul Johnson, the former editor of the 'New Statesman' and an historian and broadcaster, 'Religion is too important a matter to leave to the clergy'.

Corrymeela has this message, and its strength lies in the number of lay people and young people who are seeing the distinctive role of the Christian layman not only in the Church, but in society in general.

Another practical contribution of Corrymeela is its bridge building in a society that has become accustomed to destruction. Corrymeela has been the kind of organization that has allowed people from both sides to meet one another, without any strings attached. The lack of communication across the divide

107

in Northern Ireland has been catastrophic. Politicians and churchmen have their image to preserve, they have their roles to play. So often there has been no real meeting of mind with mind, or heart with heart, or person with person. Each has his mask, his stereotype, his political or ecclesiastical idolatry to preserve. Yet the only way to destroy the stereotypes, to cast away the idols and to penetrate behind the masks has been to enable people to meet on neutral ground as people, to get them to talk and to listen and to look behind the facades to the real person so very like oneself. When this happens, then real talk, real recreation, real dialogue can take place. Revel Howe in his book 'The Miracle of Dialogue' writes: 'Every man is a potential adversary, even those whom we love. Only through dialogue are we saved from this emnity toward one another. Dialogue is to love, what blood is to the body. When the flow of blood stops, the body dies. When dialogue stops, love dies and resentment and hate are born. But dialogue can restore a dead relationship. Indeed this is the miracle of dialogue; it can bring relationship into being, and it can bring into being once again a relationship that has died. There is only one qualification to these claims for dialogue; it must be mutual and proceed from both sides, and the parties to it must persist relentlessly. The word of dialogue may be spoken by one side but evaded or ignored by the other, in which case the promise may not be fulfilled. There is risk in speaking the dialogical words—that is, in entering into dialogue—but when two persons undertake it and accept their fear of doing so, the miracle-working power of dialogue may be released'.

Corrymeela has tried to achieve this. It is difficult to explain exactly how. Perhaps it is a combination of the beautiful natural setting on the County Antrim coast, the relaxed atmosphere, the spirit of openness and acceptance and the background of the community of people who believe that God, the God-spell, the God-force is really alive. Many different individuals and groups have spoken of this intangible in their own way.

Another contribution of Corrymeela has been the rediscovery of the sheer simplicity and power of the Gospel story. This has emerged repeatedly in the joint-worship meetings at Corrymeela. Different families from the troubled areas of Belfast—families who would not and could not meet elsewhere—came together at Corrymeela and they listened to the story of that remarkable and charismatic Christ figure. Each story in their joint worship was listened to and understood because the language of Christ had been spoken for ordinary people. These meetings were reminders that Christ's first hearers were just such people, unsophisticated, relatively poor and socially disorientated. On one occasion the children did a mime about the Good Samaritan and everybody got the point that Christ's Palestine was divided and troubled, just like Ireland, with Jewish 'Protestants' and Samaritan 'Roman Catholics'. At times it was almost possible to actually see the comfort and strength and the hope that came to the weary and worn parents from the city ghettos as the familiar words of Christ came to them with the fresh meaning 'Come unto me all you who labour and are heavy laden, and I will give you rest'.

On the beautiful North Antrim coast

At such times it was possible to understand how often the people of the Christian faith had insulated themselves from the searing, challenging, disturbing reality and dynamic of Christ by hiding behind elaborate theology and ecclesiastical language and structures. Christ spoke profoundly, but simply. And the ordinary people heard the message, and at Corrymeela.

But Corrymeela has not just been about the language of communication. The theology of Corrymeela has not just been talked about, it has been lived. Corrymeela at its best has tried to be a combination of both, an inner questioning allied to hard work and practical help.

So Corrymeela has not just talked about the problems of violence, or mixed marriages, or one-parent families, or the media and conflict. It has brought different groups together, it has tried to create dialogue and, most important, to keep that dialogue going when the delegates from each group have gone back home. And yet, despite the achievements, how far is Corrymeela a success? It has never claimed to be a success story. Corrymeela does not think of success in conventional terms. Certainly Corrymeela has its limitations. In one sense it has failed to project itself to the mass of people in Ireland. It is known for its work in taking people away from the troubled areas, but so often this is where the understanding about Corrymeela falls short. It is regarded by many still as a kind of 'clean living' holiday camp. The deeper significance and the challenge of the whole Corrymeela venture is still to be projected on a wider scale.

Corrymeela is also limited in its numbers. It still has only a small core of people directly involved, though its adherents and supporters now number thousands. But partly because of its lack of full-time workers Corrymeela has a certain lack of professionalism, which kindly observers gloss over as 'Irish charm', but which other professionals find maddening. And yet Corrymeela comes through as only it can. An example of this was the conference on media and conflict. Before the meeting, a number of senior journalists and broadcasters had grave doubts about the efficacy of the exercise. Some feared it would be at worst a shambles, at best an irrelevance. In practice, it became one of the more successful conferences with a fair proportion of the media men finding a new dimension to themselves and to their subjects which those battle-weary commentators had not thought possible.

Corrymeela also faces the danger of limitations in its concept. Or to be more accurate, certain people who regard themselves as part of the Community, are in danger of compromising Corrymeela. There is a 'trendiness' in having been to Corrymeela and having met with some of those who think that they are ahead of the religious field. Corrymeela is a difficult and a risky conception, and those who limit their vision to that of what Corrymeela can do for them are missing entirely the main ethos of the Community.

Given its limitations, and they are very human limitations, Corrymeela has been a success. Its success, (to use a word that is frowned upon by the Corrymeela Community) has the mark of a supra-human quality. Corrymeela and what it symbolizes could not be the work of men and women alone. Even to the most sceptical outside observer Corrymeela has 'something'. Outsiders would not call it Christianity, they might not try to give it any label, but the true Corrymeela has a simplicity, an honesty and a freshness that stands out in the complexity, dishonesty and the stagnation of the society in which it was conceived. Other critics point to its apparent naiveté, its hope in the middle of so many signs of communal hatred, decay and doom; and yet there is more than a lingering suspicion that the people of Corrymeela are finding in their difficult and perplexing work, an inner peace that the world alone cannot give.

Of course there are tensions. The membership includes a wide variety of people with different outlooks, hopes and commitments. There is a clash between the radicals and the conservatives, there is a clash between those who are more involved and those who are less involved in the work of Corrymeela itself. There have been the mistakes and the failures and the tensions of trying new ways. Yet the very existence of tension is a sign of life, of movement, and of change. Corrymeela is a microcosm of society itself. Corrymeela's searching for identity, its communal challenge and its ultimate striving for individual inner peace is not easy to portray. That kind of new thinking around the Christ person and the Christ challenge was summarized in a highly individual way by the actor and broadcaster Tom Fleming who gave a thoughtful talk in a BBC epilogue series called 'My Jesus'. And yet Fleming's interpretation would not be out of place in a place like Corrymeela. He said: 'An actor has to be a clinical creature. He has to reject the received image of a character and dig deep for motive and the mechanism of what makes a person tick. Jesus under such scrutiny is unpredictable, bewildering sometimes, surprising always. His wisdom and the clarity of his daylight will not be compromised by religion or what we choose to call morality or respectability. He doesn't appeal to "certain kinds" of people—the old, the susceptible, the emotional. He rarely appeals at all. He confronts. He drives out content for ever and replaces it with joy. He drives out ease of body and of mind and replaces it with the claim of impossible demands— with the needs of a whole world. The phrase "My Jesus" is a nonsense. I would never seek a creation of my own imagining for my best friend. I would not cherish the friendship of a person compounded of my own selection of available myth and legend. I value the friendship of Jesus because such friendship brings some purpose to the struggle that life is, brings something that approaches meaning to suffering, gives a view of death that fills every moment of life with a unique and unpreservable sweetness all its own. But perhaps most important of all, amid all the confusion and bewilderment, and the seeming utter failure of so much one tried to do, He brings a peace that somehow, despite everything, survives.'

Corrymeela itself survives, but what of the future? It is here that the Community contains the seeds of its further development or its decay. Corrymeela's strength has been its openness, its flexibility, its adaptability, and its ability to act quickly when necessary and to change plans at short notice. But Corrymeela's growth and success inherently challenges this openness. An organization can be flexible when it is small, but increasing size presupposes discipline and bureaucracy.

And so often bureaucracy leads to fossilization. Corrymeela is a protest movement, but the problems of protest movements are very real. Some make their protest and when their point has been taken they fade away. Today's radicals so often become yesterday's men. Will Corrymeela, and successive Corrymeela people, continually see the point and adapt accordingly?

Corrymeela has been mainly about reconciliation. Its most obvious problem has been the reconciliation in Ireland between Roman Catholics and Protestants, between two cultures, two religions, two tribes, two attitudes to life. Corrymeela has ploughed a difficult furrow, but with the hindsight of history this may be seen to have been its easier path. The issues have been direct. They have been the failures of Church and State and of Irish society itself. Corrymeela was in a position to try to say something about Ireland, to make noises about Irish society, and to try to do something. The candle flickering in the darkness attracts greater attention than a battery of lights in the bright sunlight.

Corrymeela's biggest test may be in the future, when peace comes to Ireland. Its challenge is that mentioned by Arnold Toynbee in 'A Study of History' when he concludes that a culture survives in proportion to its ability to respond to the demands of the age. The issues in Ireland have been sharp and Corrymeela has been tested. When peace comes, Corrymeela once again will need to prepare itself for a new situation.

It is important, too, to remember that Corrymeela did not come into existence because of the 'Troubles' in

Ireland. In a sense the Irish conflict was an interruption to Corrymeela's work. In 1965 its founder-members were asking the same questions about change, and what could be done about it. They discussed the kind of society that had to be worked for, and then the Irish violence came and demonstrated not only the need for change but the certainty of change.

So in war and peace the same fundamental questions will remain to challenge Corrymeela. There is the challenge of the plural society, not only in Ireland but in the world at large. It has become almost a ritual to stress that the Irish situation is unique. But it is no more unique than the situation in Cyprus or the Middle East, or in parts of America, Africa or Asia where hatred and intolerance crowd out reason and understanding. The problem of 'them' and 'us' is not just that of Irish Catholics or Protestants. It is the 'them' and 'us' of Belfast, or Birmingham, or Baltimore, or Alabama, or Sharpeville or Seoul. What happens between misunderstanding people in Ireland is relevant to misunderstanding in the rest of the world. The Irish situation has been a test case for the Christian message. The Corrymeela message has been this—can the Christian message break through the structures, political, social and ecclesiastical, that imprison society in general, and in so doing bring liberation and hope for every man and woman? This international challenge will continue to be Corrymeela's challenge, what ever happens in Ireland.

Corrymeela's challenge is also localized. One of the great dangers facing the Corrymeela people is that of forming a spiritual élite. There is always the comfort of speaking with like-minded people, of feeling that your own group has a particularly relevant message, of believing that the Establishment, the churches, the church people, are inevitably slow and totally out of touch. Such thinking leads to élitism. And if Corrymeela becomes an élitist ghetto it will become, as the Rev. Carlisle Patterson pointed out in a most challenging talk at a Retreat, no longer God's 'question-mark' but a 'full stop'.

It is the role of Christians to try to understand what God is saying in the current situation. Corrymeela is not a substitute for the churches nor has it ever claimed to be so. Nor has it ever claimed to be the only reconciliation group in Ireland. Corrymeela has not tried to smooth out the differences. It has tried to accept differences and to talk frankly about them. Corrymeela has been described as the place where you don't have to whisper. Its greater task of reconciliation needs to be worked out locally, not just at Corrymeela. Reconciliation has to be achieved through people who can never come physically to Corrymeela. Reconciliation has to be achieved by involvement in local churches and community centres however dull or forbidding these may seem to be by comparison. The real work for Corrymeela in the future may be less glamorous, less direct, less obvious than in the past. It will need even greater determination, clarity of purpose and Christian commitment.

Ray Davey, that remarkable man, who has been so much in himself Corrymeela, is already looking to the future. 'The new society must be based on social justice on the recognition of the dignity and worth of every person. It must eliminate all that cheapens and depersonalizes the human being. This is no new idea.

This is what the word peace meant to the people who used it in the Bible. The whole concept of the biblical word "Shalom" puts our insipid word "peace" into the shade. We need to have a big concept of God and of his mission of "Shalom" for the whole world. Corrymeela exists to proclaim this. Can the many good people in the churches and the many good people outside the churches who cannot find their place within because of what we haven't done and been, God forgive us, can all these people join with us to work for a different society?

'If we all, whether in Corrymeela or not, can look to this kind of future, then what Corrymeela has tried to do may not have been in vain. Perhaps some day someone will write of us like the author who inscribed these words on the porch of an English village church at the height of that country's terrible civil war: 'In the year 1642, when most things sacred were either demolished or profaned, this church was built by one whose singular praise it is to have done the best things in the worst times, and to have hoped them in the most calamitous''.'

In the final analysis, Corrymeela is not about big words, or grandiose gestures, it is about help and challenge to simple folk in the sense that all men and women deep in their hearts can be simple folk if they so choose. Corrymeela simply and humbly is about a letter from one of the Corrymeela workers to Harold Good, the Ballycastle Director. The worker wrote: 'I enclose copies of the few letters received by Mrs. Black after a visit to Corrymeela. I thought that the staff would like to see them and of course I count them as further evidence that there is a rich return to be obtained when the most unlikely people meet. It is interesting to note that the kids who wrote are all from the Orange side of the "big gulf" and Mrs. Black has told me that some of them have arranged to meet her in the city centre. She herself can hardly read so it is really illuminating that "Prod" kids on a school exercise should react so warmly to an elderly, scarcely literate, Roman Catholic woman whose son was killed by Protestants, and that she in turn should accept their friendship so joyfully. She has told me that she will never go back to Corrymeela as the pain of leaving it was too great'.

That, more than words alone can convey, is Corrymeela in action. And on the dark days when the war clouds gather and darkness overshadows the humanity of man and the faith even of believers is stretched almost beyond endurance, there are still the rich, revealing and quiet moments when the motto of Corrymeela shines through: 'It is better to light a candle than to curse the darkness'.

And somehow, that light lingers on.

ACKNOWLEDGMENTS

Grateful acknowledgment is made to the Division of Education of the National Council of Churches of Christ in the USA for the quotations from the *Revised Standard Version*; to *The Month* for the quotation from an article by Tony Spencer; to The Saint Andrew Press for the quotation from *The Miracle of Dialogue* by Revel Howe; to the British Broadcasting Corporation for the quotation from Tom Fleming's *Epilogue* talk; to Faber & Faber for the quotation from Professor J.C. Beckett's *The Making of Modern Ireland*; to *The Belfast Telegraph* and to *The Sunday Independent* for various quotations and for the use of drawings by Rowel Friers; to Dr. John Greer for the quotation from his paper, *A Questing Generation*; to The Iona Community for the quotation from *Only One Way Left* by George F. MacLeod; to Penguin Press for the quotation from *A History of Modern Ireland* by Dr. Edward Norman; to Routledge & Kegan Paul for the background from *The Shaping of Modern Ireland* edited by Dr. C.C. O'Brien; to Hutchinson for the quotation from *States of Ireland* by Dr. C.C. O'Brien; to Geoffrey Chapman for the background from *Drums and Guns Revolution in Ulster* by Martin Wallace; to Blackstaff Press for the quotation from *Northern Ireland 1968-73, a Chronology of Events* by Richard Deutsch and Vivien Magowan; to Pro Mundi Vita for the quotation from *The Irish Conflict and the Christian Conscience* by Father Patrick Daigan; and to *The Belfast Newsletter* for the quotation from *Don't Fence Me In* by R.R. Davey.